James Weldon Johnson

Twayne's United States Authors Series

David J. Nordloh, Editor

Indiana University, Bloomington

TUSAS 530

JAMES WELDON JOHNSON
(1871–1938)
Photograph by Carl Van Vechten

James Weldon Johnson

By Robert E. Fleming

University of New Mexico

Twayne Publishers
A Division of G.K. Hall & Co. • Boston

James Weldon Johnson

Robert E. Fleming

Copyediting supervised by Lewis DeSimone
Book production by Marne B. Sultz
Book design by Barbara Anderson

Typeset in 11 pt. Garamond
by P&M Typesetting, Inc., Waterbury, Connecticut

Printed on permanent/durable acid-free paper
and bound in the United States of America

Library of Congress Cataloging in Publication Data

Fleming, Robert E. (Robert Edward), 1936–
    James Weldon Johnson.

    (Twayne's United States authors series ; TUSAS 530)
    Bibliography: p. 117
    Includes index.
    1. Johnson, James Weldon, 1871–1938—Criticism and
interpretation.   2. Afro-Americans in literature.
3. Harlem Renaissance.   I.   Title. II. Series.
PS3519.02625Z67   1987   818'.5209   86-31824
ISBN 0-8057-7491-2 (alk. paper)

To Esther

Contents

About the Author

Robert E. Fleming is Professor of English at the University of New Mexico, where he has taught since completing his Ph.D. at the University of Illinois. He is also the author of *Willard Motley* in Twayne's United States Authors Series and of *James Weldon Johnson and Arna Wendell Bontemps: A Reference Guide* and *Sinclair Lewis: A Reference Guide*, published by G.K. Hall. His essays on nineteenth- and twentieth-century American literature have appeared in such journals as *American Literature*, *Arizona Quarterly*, *Black American Literature Forum*, *Contemporary Literature*, *CLA Journal*, *Hemingway Review*, *MidAmerica*, *Modern Fiction Studies*, *Phylon*, and *Studies in American Fiction*.

Preface

Assessing the place of James Weldon Johnson in modern Afro-American letters is in some ways similar to weighing the influence of Ezra Pound on modern poetry. Johnson's contributions are more significant than the sum of his works might seem to indicate. The model that he provided younger writers and the advice that he gave them in his critical articles and prefaces have had incalculable effects that continue even yet.

Johnson was truly the "renaissance man" of the Harlem Renaissance. Brought up and educated conservatively, he nevertheless fit into the avant-garde black literary movement that marked the Harlem of the 1920s and in fact he became its elder statesman. As a novelist he transcended the melodramatic conventions that had dominated the black novel from William Wells Brown's day past the turn of the century; and by replacing those conventions with more sophisticated techniques such as an unreliable narrator and subtle irony, he opened up new possibilities for black novelists through the middle of the twentieth century. As a poet he soon recognized the limitations of the formal diction of nineteenth-century poetry and the outmoded conventions of dialect poetry; his search for a more satisfactory form and language ended with a flexible free verse that presents black speech both more accurately and more poetically than the dialect he had left behind. His critical essays and prefaces provided a perspective on the past as well as direction for the future for black writers during the 1920s and 1930s.

In the first chapter of this book I present the forces that made Johnson the writer he was, from the early examples of his parents and certain teachers to his later experiences as teacher, principal, lawyer, newspaperman, songwriter, diplomat, and executive of the National Association for the Advancement of Colored People. Succeeding chapters treat his achievements as novelist, poet, critic, historian, political activist, and autobiographer. While Johnson's social message was always important to him, I have attempted to show, particularly in the second and third chapters, that he was also a conscious stylist who broke new ground in the arts of fiction and poetry.

I wish to thank David E. Schoonover, Curator of the Collection of

American Literature, Beinecke Rare Book Room and Manuscript Library, Yale University, for allowing me access to the James Weldon Johnson Collection. I thank Marta Field, of the Department of English, University of New Mexico, for typing the several stages of the manuscript. For financial support I am indebted to the Research Allocations Committee of the University of New Mexico. Finally, and most important, I thank my wife Esther and my daughter Kathleen for their patience, support, and encouragement while I worked on the book.

Robert E. Fleming

University of New Mexico

Acknowledgments

I wish to thank the following for permission to quote from the works listed:

From *The Book of American Negro Spirituals,* edited by James Weldon Johnson. Copyright 1925, 1926 by the Viking Press, Inc. Copyright renewed © 1953 by Grace Nail Johnson, J. Rosamond Johnson, and Lawrence Brown. Copyright renewed © 1954 by Grace Nail Johnson and J. Rosamond Johnson. Reprinted by permission of Viking Penguin Inc.

From *Negro Americans, What Now?* by James Weldon Johnson. Copyright 1934 by James Weldon Johnson. Copyright renewed © 1962 by Grace Nail Johnson. Reprinted by permission of Viking Penguin Inc.

From *God's Trombones* by James Weldon Johnson. Copyright 1927 by James Weldon Johnson. Copyright renewed © 1955 by Grace Nail Johnson. Reprinted by permission of Viking Penguin Inc.

From *St. Peter Relates an Incident: Selected Poems* by James Weldon Johnson. Copyright 1935 by James Weldon Johnson. Copyright renewed © 1963 by Grace Nail Johnson. Reprinted by permission of Viking Penguin Inc.

From *Along This Way* by James Weldon Johnson. Copyright 1933 by James Weldon Johnson. Copyright renewed © 1961 by Grace Nail Johnson. Reprinted by permission of Viking Penguin Inc.

From *The Book of American Negro Poetry,* edited by James Weldon Johnson, copyright 1922, 1931 by Harcourt, Brace Jovanovich, Inc.; renewed 1950 by Grace Johnson, 1959 by Mrs. Grace Nail Johnson. Reprinted by permission of the publisher.

From *The Autobiography of an Ex-Coloured Man* by James Weldon Johnson. Copyright 1912 by James Weldon Johnson. Copyright © 1960 by Hill & Wang. Reprinted by permission of Hill & Wang.

From *Black Manhattan* by James Weldon Johnson, copyright 1930. Copyright renewed © 1958 Mrs. James Weldon Johnson. Reprinted with the permission of Charles Scribner's Sons.

Thanks to the Collection of American Literature, Beinecke Rare Book

Room and Manuscript Library, Yale University, for permission to quote from Johnson's working notes and scrapbooks.

Parts of chapter 2 previously appeared in *American Literature* 43 (1971) and are published by permission of that journal and of Duke University Press.

Frontispiece appears by courtesy of the Estate of Carl Van Vechten, Joseph Solomon, Executor, and the Collection of American Literature, Beinecke Rare Book Room and Manuscript Library, Yale University.

Chronology

1871   James William Johnson born 17 June in Jacksonville, Florida. (In 1913 he changes his middle name to Weldon.)

1887   Graduates from Stanton School, Jacksonville; enrolls in preparatory school at Atlanta University.

1894   Graduates from Atlanta University; becomes principal of Stanton School, Jacksonville.

1895   Founds a newspaper, the *Daily American,* in Jacksonville.

1898   Admitted to the Florida bar.

1900   Writes "Lift Every Voice and Sing" with his brother Rosamond.

1902   Leaves Jacksonville for New York to become a writer of songs and musical comedies with Rosamond and their partner, Bob Cole.

1904   Receives honorary M.A. degree from Atlanta University. Active in Colored Republican Club in New York.

1906   Takes charge of U.S. Consulate, Puerto Cabello, Venezuela.

1909   Takes charge of U.S. Consulate, Corinto, Nicaragua.

1910   10 February, marries Grace Nail.

1912   Publishes *The Autobiography of an Ex-Colored Man* anonymously.

1913   Publishes "Fifty Years."

1914   Resigns from Consular Service. Becomes contributing editor of the *New York Age.*

1916   Becomes field secretary of the NAACP.

1917   *Fifty Years and Other Poems.*

1920   Becomes secretary of the NAACP.

1922   Edits *The Book of American Negro Poetry.*

1925   Edits *The Book of American Negro Spirituals.*

1926   Edits *The Second Book of American Negro Spirituals.*

1927   Republication of Johnson's novel as *The Autobiography of an Ex-Coloured Man*. *God's Trombones*.

1930   *Black Manhattan; St. Peter Relates An Incident* (small private edition). Resigns as secretary of the NAACP.

1931   Revised and enlarged edition of *The Book of American Negro Poetry*.

1932   Accepts teaching position at Fisk University.

1933   *Along This Way*.

1934   *Negro Americans, What Now?*

1935   *St. Peter Relates an Incident: Selected Poems*.

1938   26 June, dies in an automobile accident near Wiscasset, Maine.

Chapter One

Breaking the Limitations of Race

When James William Johnson was born in 1871, the Emancipation Proclamation was less than ten years old. By the time he began to write his first book, he had already experienced both the advantages and disadvantages of the turbulent era that followed Reconstruction. Granted educational opportunities that were excellent for his day, Johnson had made the most of them, publishing articles and poems while a student at Atlanta University, returning to Jacksonville to found a black newspaper, serving as a public school principal, and winning admission to the Florida bar. But he had also been subjected to the resistance against more equitable treatment of black Americans: riding between Jacksonville and Atlanta in the Jim Crow cars of trains, facing the unreasonable opposition of one of his examiners at the bar examination, and nearly being shot by a white National Guardsman during a period of martial law in Jacksonville. It was experiences like these as much as the formal education Johnson received that would shape most of his literary works in the years that followed.

Jacksonville Boyhood

Johnson was born 17 June 1871, in Jacksonville, Florida. His parents were James Johnson, headwaiter at the Saint James Hotel, a major resort in Jacksonville, and Helen Dillet Johnson, who taught school for some twenty years at Jacksonville's all-black Stanton School. Neither of Johnson's parents had experienced slavery. James Johnson had been born a freeman in Virginia and had moved to New York City before the Civil War, and Helen Dillet, the well-educated daughter of a prominent family from Nassau, had grown up free in the Bahamas, where slavery had been outlawed since 1833, and later in New York City. Both enthusiastically joined the rising black middle class of Jacksonville, buying a large lot with a ramshackle house, which James Johnson soon replaced. James Weldon Johnson remembered the house years later as the most elaborate in the neighborhood, with three bedrooms, parlor, and kitchen, fronted with a broad piazza, and surrounded by a yard landscaped with maple and orange trees. His brother, John Rosamond, who would be his collaborator in musical-comedy writing and song collecting, was born two years after James.

If his living conditions were considerably better than those of most black youths of his time, Johnson's cultural advantages were even greater. Before he was six years old, he had been to New York City and to Nassau. His parents' home held many books, and years later he remembered his mother reading *David Copperfield* aloud to him when he was only five or six years of age. He also remembered reading for himself, while he was still quite young, works such as *Pickwick Papers, Pilgrim's Progress,* and both fiction and poetry by Sir Walter Scott.[1] Helen Johnson was a competent if not inspired pianist, and Johnson and his brother Rosamond were both taught how to play at an early age. Finally, Mrs. Johnson had artistic interests as well: Johnson remembered his mother's drawing during his youth, and when he was in his teens, she "revealed to me that she had written verse, and showed me a thin sheaf of poems copied out in her almost perfect handwriting" (A, 11).

From his father Johnson learned the solid virtues of honesty and dependability. James Johnson had been self-educated and was less an intellectual influence on Johnson than his mother. Yet Johnson prized a copy of *Plutarch's Lives* left to him by his father, and recalled that his father had taught himself Spanish to further his career as a headwaiter. The elder Johnson had attended the theater regularly as a young man in New York and used to recite speeches from Shakespeare's plays to his sons. Although Johnson saw far less of his father than of his mother because of the long hours his father worked at the hotel, he was nevertheless influenced by his example.

An early influence that did not prove so long-lasting as that of his parents was the religion to which Johnson's maternal grandmother introduced him. While he was growing up, his parents were not overly religious, although his father would later become a lay minister in the Baptist faith.[2] The boy's grandmother sought to remedy this deficiency by taking her grandson with her to the Ebenezer Methodist Episcopal Church and by reading Bible stories to him at home. Her greatest ambition for Johnson was to make a preacher of him (A, 25). Johnson responded to the pressure to be "saved" when he was nine years old, at a revival meeting. After several evenings of attendance with his grandmother, he remembered that

> I was led to the mourners' bench. I knelt down at the altar. I was so wedged in that I could hardly breathe. I tried to pray. I tried to feel a conviction of sin. I, finally, fell asleep. . . . The meeting was about to close; somebody shook me by the shoulder. . . . I woke up but did not open my eyes or stir. . . . Whence sprang the whim, as cunning as could have occurred to one of the devil's own imps? The shaking continued, but I neither opened my eyes nor stirred. They gathered round me. I heard, "Glory to God, the child's gone off!" (*A*, 26)

After being carried home by one of the men of the congregation, Johnson appeared to awaken and told his grandmother of a vision, for which he drew on the Bible stories she had read him. His pleased grandmother declared the boy "saved." For some time, he remained a member of his grandmother's church, absorbing the details of revival meetings, the rhetoric of black preachers, and the sound of the spirituals, which he would later help to preserve. But by the time he was a freshman at Atlanta University, Johnson was one of two students in his class who confessed his agnosticism.

He learned to read early and was proficient by the time he entered the Stanton School, where he was a good student, though by no means outstanding. He later reflected that, since he had already been taught a great deal at home, he should have graduated from the eighth grade in the spring before his thirteenth birthday, but actually he was just short of sixteen when he graduated (*A*, 61). But Stanton offered other advantages besides the academic life: Johnson learned to mix with other children and played baseball with some distinction, learning to pitch a curve ball. When he graduated from the eighth grade, he had exhausted the educational opportunities open to him in Jacksonville and had to look elsewhere for a high school education. After considering Howard University, Fisk, Atlanta, Biddle University, and Hampton Institute, the family council decided that Johnson would attend the preparatory school connected with Atlanta University.

Better and Nobler

The university to which he traveled in the fall of 1887 was an idealistic institution founded in 1869 by the American Missionary Asso-

ciation to provide a high school education and normal school training
for black southern students.[3] Staffed largely by white New England
teachers, the school held up high ideals to its students. As Johnson
summed up the school's credo in *Along This Way,*

> The conception of education then held there and at other Negro colleges be-
> longed to an age that, probably, is passing never to return. The central idea
> embraced a term that is now almost a butt for laughter—"service." We were
> never allowed to entertain any thought of being educated as "go-getters."
> Most of us knew that we were being educated for life work as underpaid
> teachers. The ideal constantly held up to us was of education as a means of
> living, not of making a living. It was impressed upon us that taking a classi-
> cal course would have an effect of making us better and nobler, and of higher
> value to those we should have to serve. An odd, old-fashioned, naïve concep-
> tion? Rather. (*A*, 122)

Paradoxically, it was on his way to one of the day's leading black
colleges that Johnson first encountered blatant racial discrimination.
Riding in the first-class car of the train to Atlanta with a swarthy
Cuban friend who was also to attend the university, Johnson was
warned by the conductor to move to the Jim Crow car. When his
friend asked Johnson in Spanish what was wrong and Johnson answered in the same language, the conductor assumed that the two
were foreign and let them keep their seats, leading Johnson to conclude that "in such situations any kind of a Negro will do; provided
he is not one who is an American citizen" (*A*, 65). Although Johnson
evaded the Jim Crow law on this occasion, on the way home from his
first year at Atlanta he and some companions were moved from the
first-class to the Jim Crow car by the threat of violence (*A*, 84–86).

Johnson's first year at the Atlanta University preparatory school
widened his horizons in a number of ways. He soon noticed that even
the younger boys gracefully took the floor to speak and debate publicly: oratory was a highly respected accomplishment at Atlanta. Rec-
ognizing that he was comparatively inept as a public speaker, he
joined the debating society and worked hard at public speaking during his first year, achieving considerable success and laying the
groundwork for future careers. He began to read more widely, taking
advantage of the college library to acquaint himself with further novels by Dickens as well as with George Eliot's novels, William Make-
peace Thackeray's *Vanity Fair,* and Richard Blackmore's *Lorna Doone.*
He also turned his hand to poetry for the first time, his output ranging from humorous verse to love poems.

The summer of 1888 brought an epidemic of yellow fever to Jacksonville, and when it was time for Johnson to return for his second year at Atlanta, he was still under quarantine. As it became obvious that he would lose the school year, Johnson began to look for a tutor. His father suggested a black West Indian cobbler who had a reputation for scholarship; to Johnson's surprise, the man whom he found in a small, unprosperous shop was a fine teacher. With this shoemaker Johnson studied Latin and Greek throughout the 1888–89 school year. He also found intellectual stimulation of a different sort when he applied for a job as receptionist to a physician, Dr. T. O. Summers. Summers brought a cosmopolitan air to Jacksonville. He had traveled widely through Europe, the Near East, and Africa as well as the United States and was fluent in French and German. He enjoyed a local reputation as a poet, publishing in the *Times-Union.* Best of all, he had a library that surpassed that of Atlanta University in the intellectual freedom it represented, if not in the number of volumes. Working for Summers, Johnson read Boccaccio and Balzac in addition to Thomas Paine's *Age of Reason* and Robert Ingersoll's *Some Mistakes of Moses* and *The Gods and Other Lectures.* Johnson's year off was so productive that on his return to Atlanta for the 1889–90 school year he felt confident enough to petition for permission to do two years of prepararory work in one. Permission was granted, and he was ready to matriculate into the freshman class at Atlanta in the fall of 1890.

Johnson's four years as a college student at Atlanta gave him a solid education with an emphasis on Latin and Greek but with adequate attention to more modern and useful studies such as mathematics, English, and science. He worked all four years in the university printing office and thus learned practical lessons that would be of use in his later careers in journalism and editing. It was in the printing office that he was first introduced to Booker T. Washington, who had come to visit the Atlanta school (*A,* 101–2). Before his graduation he heard Frederick Douglass speak at the Columbian Exposition in Chicago, where he also met Paul Laurence Dunbar, already a published poet.[4]

Another important practical experience was teaching in a rural school in Henry County, Georgia, during the summer of 1891. The job paid more in experience than in cash, for as Johnson remembered it years later, his pay was five cents per day for each pupil in the class. What Johnson learned, however, was how poor black farmers lived in Georgia. He boarded with a family that was probably better off than most, yet the family had only a two-room cabin, one room of which was allotted to the teacher. The fastidious Johnson was appalled by the farmers' diet, which was primarily greens and cornbread. He lamented the absence of bathing facilities and the lack of good light by which to study in the evenings. School was held in the local church, where the pupils sat on rough benches. Johnson treated his experience humorously in a letter home to Rosamond, poking fun at the board of trustees, whose members he had to consult regularly: "The Chairman of the Board was undoubtedly intended by nature for a smart man. He has a very strong weakness for using big words in the wrong place and thinks it his special duty to impress the 'fesser at all times with his knowledge of the dictionary."[5] He included in the same letter a bit of light verse and a semifictional anecdote about the tribulations he suffered when he had to depend on a Georgia mule for transportation.

Thus, during the summer of 1891 Johnson gained a new understanding of a class that had previously been outside his personal experience. Years later, his most vivid memories were of one student, "Tunk" Laster, about whom he wrote a poem. Tunk's attitude toward education illustrates the difficulties Johnson faced with at least some of his pupils:

I became interested in him the first day of school, when I found out that although it was his third term he had failed to master the alphabet. I wondered how he had managed to perform such a feat and I determined to make him break the series. . . . I devoted my best personal effort to "Tunk" throughout the whole term, and I made the easy discovery that by the time he got slightly familiar with X, Y, Z, he had forgotten all about A, B, C. . . . "Tunk" was not stupid; he had consciously or unconsciously made up his mind that he wasn't going to study. Neither old-fashioned nor modern methods made any impression on him. (A, 111)

Johnson returned to his teaching post after his second year at Atlanta.

Not all of his important experiences at Atlanta University were academic. He continued to be active in the debating society and in 1892 won the Quiz Club's prize for oratory with a speech on "The Best Methods of Removing the Disabilities of Caste from the Negro."[6] He was also active in the glee club and accompanied it on a fund-raising tour through New England in the summer following his graduation. He continued to write: four poems and two prose pieces—the latter first delivered as orations—were published in the *Atlanta University*

Bulletin. Although his career would contain some detours, Johnson had begun a literary apprenticeship.

Educator

When Johnson graduated from Atlanta University, President Horace Bumstead offered to help him get a scholarship to attend Harvard Medical School. However, at the same time another opportunity presented itself in the resignation of William Artrell, the principal of Stanton School in Jacksonville. In the fall of 1894 Johnson, whose sole teaching experience was his two summers in rural Georgia, became principal of his old grammar school in charge of one thousand pupils and twenty-five teachers. Not content merely to maintain the status quo at Stanton, he soon began to study ways of improving the school. To generate ideas for improvement, he obtained permission to visit Jacksonville's grammar school, where he spent half a day visiting classes. Later he discovered that white parents nearly caused a racial incident when they heard of the visit. Only the testimony of the school superintendent and the principal of the white school that Johnson had had permission for his visit caused the affair to die down without violence (*A*, 126–27).

At the end of his first academic year as principal, Johnson conceived a major improvement in the school. Seeing his graduating class of twenty-six students receive their eighth-grade diplomas, he determined to make it possible for them to obtain further education without leaving home to go to a prep school as he had had to do some eight years before. He spoke to the students and their parents over the summer, and in the fall of 1895 he personally began to teach a ninth-grade course modeled closely on the first year of studies at the Atlanta University preparatory school. At the end of the school year he informed the school superintendent of what he had done and then asked for an assistant so that he could add a tenth year of schooling. Thus he was able to add two years of high school education within his first three years as principal.

Disappointment with the job set in, however, when Johnson reflected that he had begun at the top of the ladder. As a teacher and principal in Jacksonville, he had nowhere else to go. The best he could look forward to was a lifetime of service in a position that, in spite of the considerable responsibility it entailed, was poorly paid. When Stanton School burned down in a disastrous fire that swept

Jacksonville in 1901, Johnson and his brother rushed to the school's office and loaded the most important records onto bicycles. While the school was being rebuilt, Johnson was in New York with Rosamond, and when he returned, he had clearly lost enthusiasm for his job as principal. Nevertheless, he rendered his old school one final service. A large ramshackle building had been thrown up on the site of the old school because the board of education had decided to rebuild replacement schools elsewhere. Johnson recognized that the board's real motive was to take over the relatively valuable land on which Stanton had stood and put the new schools on less valuable property. Johnson blocked this plan by reminding the board that the property had been deeded to a special board of trustees to be used only for a Negro school. If anything else were done with the land, it was to revert to the heirs of Governor Hart, the donor. After checking the legal records, the board reversed its decision to relocate Stanton School.[7] In the fall of 1902 Johnson, who had been working with Rosamond writing songs, resigned his position at Stanton and moved to New York City.

Newspaperman and Lawyer

Even before the end of his first year as principal of Stanton, Johnson determined to embark on a second career as editor and publisher of his own daily paper. Having saved a few hundred dollars, he borrowed more money from his father and from two Atlanta University classmates, George Towns and N. W. Collier, and founded the *Daily American,* an afternoon daily serving the black people of Jacksonville. His partner and business manager was M. J. Christopher, but Johnson found enough time to do the editorial chores himself, including the writing of his daily editorial. Founded in May 1895, the paper at first was well received: "Subscriptions poured in. There were, perhaps because of curiosity to know what was going on among Negroes, quite a number of white subscribers. Congratulatory letters were written by patrons and encomiastic sermons delivered by preachers" (*A,* 139). But the early success was not to last. The *Daily American* expired some eight months after its founding, leaving Johnson with numerous debts.

However, his venture into journalism was not a complete failure. During the newspaper's brief life Johnson did a great deal to defend the rights of black people, to counter the stereotypes then being perpetuated by the plantation school and by demagogues, and to educate his readers. He summed up his goals in an early editorial: "*The Daily American* will be published chiefly in the interest of the colored people of Florida and the South. It will be its office to defend the Negro when he is oppressed, to counsel him when he errs, to applaud him when he is deserving, to condemn him when he sins. It is not its purpose however to stir up strife and hatred, but it shall have as its highest aim the promotion of better feeling and fuller understanding between the two races here in the South."[8]

Johnson worked toward his goals in various ways. When he wrote for his black audience, his admonitions resembled those of Booker T. Washington, urging the race to conduct itself with dignity: "Judging from the pitch of voice and the range of gesture of some people while on our streets, it seems as if they have the mistaken idea that streets were made solely for rough conduct. . . . All have a right to a place on the streets, but at the same time, no one should forget the fact that the streets are simply public conveniences where the rights of others should be as strictly respected as our own" (Scrapbook 1, p. 19).

But he was not content to write solely to black people about the improvement of their conduct. One of his editorial projects was to challenge the state law that made it a criminal offense to teach inte-grated classes. Johnson urged that "the colored people of the State form a fund, and take the matter into the courts" (Scrapbook 1, p. 25). In another editorial he asked, "If any white person chooses to send his child to a school where colored children are being taught, whose business is it? Has the State any right to say he shall not, espe-cially if the school is a private one, and receives no public funds[?]" (Scrapbook 1, p. 26). During his short career as editor and publisher, Johnson had an opportunity to try out his voice as racial spokesman, a role he would continue to play.

His newspaper career ended, he began to explore new avenues of bettering himself and his race. In the fall of 1896, some six months after the collapse of the *Daily American,* he approached Thomas A. Ledwith, a white Jacksonville attorney, asking if he might study law in Ledwith's office. Soon he was putting in several hours a day on school days and whole days when school was not in session. By the end of his first six months of study, Ledwith turned over most of the office paper work to him, and in another year pronounced him ready to take the bar examinations.

Although his eighteen months of study had prepared him well for the required oral examination, Johnson's admission to the bar was by no means assured. While there were a few black lawyers in Jacksonville, they had been admitted by the federal courts during Reconstruction. Johnson faced a panel of three white lawyers, presided over by a white judge. Fortunately, the judge was a man who was known to be fair to black people, but one member of the panel, Major W. B. Young, was a notorious racist. Johnson was questioned for two hours before a large audience and fielded the questions well. When it became obvious that he was passing the examination, Major Young stormed out of the room with the comment, "Well, I can't forget he's a nigger; and I'll be damned if I'll stay here to see him admitted" (A, 143). The remaining two members of the panel, however, agreed that Johnson should be admitted to the bar, and Judge R. M. Call administered the oath.

Johnson remained in his post of principal during his law practice, splitting the chores of his law partnership with an Atlanta University friend, Douglass Wetmore, who passed the bar examination some six months after Johnson. Johnson did the paper work of the office in his hours away from Stanton, and Wetmore did the court work and saw the clients. While Johnson practiced law for only a comparatively short time, his legal training was useful in later years when he served in the U.S. Foreign Service and the National Association for the Advancement of Colored People.

Johnson's legal training and ability to keep his head under pressure served him well during the period of martial law that followed the Jacksonville fire of 1901. Shortly after the fire he was approached by a woman journalist who had written an article about the effect of the fire on Jacksonville's black population and wanted Johnson to read it. She and Johnson met in Riverside Park in late afternoon and were discussing the article when a group of militiamen surprised them. The conductor and the motorman on the streetcar that had taken Johnson to the park had returned to town and reported that they had seen a black man meet a white woman in the secluded park. Some of the poorly disciplined militiamen were in favor of killing Johnson on the spot, assuming that he had broken one of the most sacred laws of the old South. But while Johnson was being cursed and struck, he maintained his composure until an officer appeared to place him under arrest. Taken before the provost marshal, another Jacksonville attorney, Johnson easily defended his case by saying, "I know there is no use in discussing law or my rights on any such basis as, 'Suppose the lady *is* white?' so I tell you at once that according to the customs and, possibly, the laws of Florida, she *is not* white" (*A,* 169). The lady promptly confirmed Johnson's statement and the provost marshal immediately understood the mistake that had been made; "Negroes" who were completely undistinguishable by their features were part of the Jacksonville scene—Johnson's partner Douglass Wetmore was a prominent example—and as Johnson observed elsewhere, in the South no white person would falsely claim Afro-American ancestry.

The Composer

In the spring of 1897 Johnson's brother Rosamond returned to Jacksonville after seven years of working in Boston, studying at the New England Conservatory of Music, and traveling with a musical comedy company. Rosamond urged Johnson to collaborate with him in writing songs and operettas, but Johnson was then studying for his bar exam while working full-time as principal of Stanton. Rosamond became a music teacher in Jacksonville and contented himself with setting a few of Johnson's poems to music, including a poem about Easter that Rosamond had sung at a Baptist church where he was choir director. In 1898, after the ordeal of the bar examination, Johnson did work with his brother on a modest musical project, an operetta performed by students as part of the graduation exercises at Stanton. Although at the time the operetta caused him nothing but trouble—a Baptist minister vigorously objected to the dancing that marked the finale—the joint project was the beginning of a fruitful collaboration that would occupy the brothers for the next seven years.

During the next year James and Rosamond worked on a comic opera, *Tolosa, or The Royal Document,* with the idea of using the work to gain entry to the world of musical comedy writing. Nor was their motive totally lighthearted: Johnson explained, "The United States had, the year before, annexed Hawaii, and was at the time engaged in the Spanish-American War. We decided to write a comic opera satirizing the new American imperialism" (*A,* 149). The opera had nothing to do with Afro-American themes. Set on an island in the Pacific, it combined a love story about an island princess and an American naval lieutenant with palace intrigues and the eventual annexation of the island. Among other things, the opera shows that

Johnson had little idea of the place to which black performers and artists of his day were relegated on the musical comedy stage.

For the most part, the black actor on the stage was limited by custom to minstrel roles; in many cases black actors, like white actors, even wore burnt-cork makeup. When a nationally recognized poet, Johnson's friend Paul Laurence Dunbar, collaborated with Will Marion Cook to produce *Clorindy, the Origin of the Cakewalk* (1897), the result was what was popularly known as a "coon show." Johnson thus described the musical situation as he found it when he arrived in New York in 1899: "The Negro songs then the rage were known as 'coon songs' and were concerned with jamborees of various sorts and the play of razors, with the gastronomical delights of chicken, pork chops and watermelon, and with the experiences of red-hot 'mammas' and their never too faithful 'papas.' These songs were for the most part crude, raucous, bawdy, often obscene" (*A,* 152–53).

The black writer, like the black actor, found himself forced into a rigid formula. Johnson set out, working with his brother and Bob Cole, a songwriter and performer whom they met on their 1899 trip to New York, to "bring a higher degree of artistry to Negro songs" (*A,* 152). That first summer the three produced and sold "Louisiana Lize" for fifty dollars, the only money the Johnsons earned from their first trip to New York, since the opera proved to be unsalable.

But the trip was not unprofitable in other ways. Besides meeting Cole and forming a working relationship with him, Johnson renewed his friendship with Paul Laurence Dunbar. He and Rosamond were introduced to notable Broadway musical figures such as Oscar Hammerstein, Harry B. Smith, Reginald DeKoven, Will Marion Cook, and Harry T. Burleigh (*A,* 150–51). Johnson returned to Jacksonville uncertain of his future plans after being exposed to the larger world of the musical comedy stage but inspired to write more. Soon after arriving in Jacksonville, he wrote his dialect poem, "Sence You Went Away," which was printed in *Century* and later set to music by Rosamond. During the 1899–1900 school year Johnson wrote a number of other dialect poems (most of which he would later describe as "trite") with the idea of turning out work appropriate for the Broadway stage. This same winter saw the production of the Johnson brothers' most famous creation. As a part of the celebration of Lincoln's birthday, Johnson wrote the words and Rosamond the music for a song that was sung by five hundred Stanton students—"Lift Every Voice and Sing." Later adopted by the NAACP, this work would eventually become known as the Negro National Anthem.

The Johnson brothers spent the summer of 1900 and the summer and fall of 1901 in New York, writing and sometimes selling songs produced by their partnership with Bob Cole. They had yet to make enough money, however, for Johnson to think of giving up his job at Stanton, and in January 1902 he returned to Jacksonville to take up his duties in the rebuilt school. At the end of the term he stayed in Jacksonville, studying for a state test for his permanent Florida teaching certificate. As he studied one day, the mail brought two letters from Rosamond, enclosing two money orders for a total of $480. Rosamond explained that their songs had begun to sell so well that their advances from their publishers were repaid, and their royalties for the first six months of 1902 were nearly $1500. Furthermore, he and Cole were a success with their vaudeville act. He urged James to join him in New York. Since the $480 represented roughly one-half of Johnson's annual salary at Stanton, he left for New York as soon as possible, though he delayed resigning his principalship until the next fall, when he was sure that he would be able to support himself in New York. The song that took Johnson to New York was "The Maiden with the Dreamy Eyes," but during his first fall as a full-time songwriter, the partners sold "Under the Bamboo Tree," which would surpass all their earlier efforts; the song was used in a popular musical called *Sally in Our Alley,* and by the middle of 1903 it had sold 400,000 copies. So successful were the last six months of 1902 that when Cole and the Johnson brothers picked up their royalty check in January 1903, they were disappointed to find that it was for slightly less than $6000. Their next semiannual royalty check was for more than $12,000, as the Johnson-Cole team entered a period of enormous popularity.

Since Johnson was the only member of the trio who did not perform on the stage, he was frequently bored when Rosamond and Bob Cole were on the road. To fill the void, he signed up for classes at Columbia University, where he studied under Professor Brander Matthews. The eclectic Matthews not only encouraged Johnson in some of his more conventional endeavors, helping him to place poems in national publications and reading the beginning of *The Autobiography of an Ex-Colored Man,* but also praised his work in musical comedy. Johnson studied part-time for three years, emphasizing English literature and drama.

Meanwhile, the Johnson brothers and Bob Cole continued to enjoy success with their songs. In 1905 they were asked to contribute several songs to the *Ladies' Home Journal,* which published four of them from May through August. But the highlight of 1905 was a six-week booking at London's Palace Theater. Johnson accompanied his brother and Bob Cole on a tour of Western Europe before going to England. The trio visited Paris, where they were surprised and pleased to hear both "Under the Bamboo Tree" and "The Congo Love Song" at the Olympia, and then moved on to other points of interest on the Continent. The engagement at the Palace was a major triumph for the Americans, and they returned to New York feeling elated.

Johnson, however, had begun to lose interest in writing songs and had misgivings about Cole and Rosamond's plans to form a theater company and tour with an original show, forsaking the successful vaudeville act with which they had toured in previous years. Moreover, Johnson felt, as he worked on *The Shoo-Fly Regiment,* the show which would inaugurate the new company, that he was marking time by writing songs and musical shows. Thus it was with considerable relief that he answered the summons of Charles W. Anderson, a black politician, to apply for a post in the U.S. Consular Service.

The Diplomat

In 1904, while Johnson was still enthusiastically pursuing his career as a songwriter, Anderson had approached him with the proposal that he serve as an officer in a "Colored Republican" club that Anderson was forming as part of the campaign to reelect President Theodore Roosevelt. Johnson was Anderson's choice, not because he was active politically, but because he combined reliability with popularity. As a favor to Anderson, whom he knew socially, Johnson accepted and, in the course of the political campaign, found himself becoming a Roosevelt supporter. With Bob Cole and Rosamond, he wrote two campaign songs, including "You're All Right, Teddy," which Roosevelt pronounced "a bully good song" (A, 219).

Once Roosevelt was in office, Anderson suggested that Johnson apply for a post in the Consular Service. At first Johnson demurred, but in 1906, feeling that it was time to move on from musical comedy, he decided to take the examination for a position. In a way, he hated to leave the New York scene, but other considerations had to be taken into account:

New York had been a good godmother to me, almost a fairy godmother, and it gave me a wrench to turn my back on her. Over against all that life and work in New York meant, I balanced three things, and they tipped the scales. I put into the scales my desire to avoid the disagreeable business of traveling round the country under the conditions that a Negro theatrical company had to endure; as I proposed to cite, among my qualifications for the Service, Spanish as my foreign language, I expected to be appointed to a South American post, so there was added the lure of the adventure of life on a strange continent; but heavier than either of these was the realization, which came upon me suddenly, that time was slipping and I had not yet made a real start on the work that I had long kept reassuring myself I should sometime do, that the opportunity for seizing that "sometime" had come, and that I ought not let it pass. (*A*, 223).

Johnson took his examination, placed well, and by 28 May 1906, had arrived at his first duty station, the consulate at Puerto Cabello, Venezuela.

In *Along This Way* Johnson nostalgically recalled the consulate fondly, although at the time he was somewhat disappointed by the shabby nature of the house that was his headquarters, and after a year he moved the consulate to a better building. One advantage of his new situation was that he had almost unlimited time to devote to his writing: his vice-consul and a clerk conducted all of the daily business of the consulate, while Johnson studied international law and wrote the official reports to Washington. In his considerable leisure time he contributed poems to *Century Magazine* and the *Independent*, finding in those journals a national audience for poems he had written while he was still in New York. He also wrote new poetry and continued to work on *The Autobiography of an Ex-Colored Man*, the novel which he had begun while taking classes from Brander Matthews. Nor did he neglect his social life during this period. Finding Venezuela completely without racial consciousness, he joined a social club of the leading men of the city and participated in activities ranging from formal dances to baseball. Finally, he devoted part of his time to correspondence that might lead to a better diplomatic post.

Although for a time Roosevelt seemed willing to appoint him to so appealing a post as Nice, France, when Johnson received his next appointment it was to Corinto, Nicaragua. He had moved up a grade and was to receive a substantially higher salary. Yet when he arrived in Corinto in 1909 he was dismayed:

My first view of Corinto sent my heart down like a plummet. What I saw was not a city or a town, but a straggling, tropical village. . . . When I got ashore, I found that the close-up was less flattering than the view from the bay. . . . It was a shanty town, built entirely of wood. There were less than a half-dozen attractive houses in it. The streets were unpaved; there was no electricity. Except for a couple of primitive grocery stores, there was not a shop in the place. (A, 255)

The new consul had to stay in one of Corinto's shabby hotels since the consulate itself was a single rented room in a private house. Even the new consulate that Johnson soon rented—the "third-best house in town" (A, 256)—was merely a three-room structure. Johnson lived in one room and had his office in another, eating his meals in a nearby hotel. Since Corinto was a busier port than Puerto Cabello, American naval vessels being anchored in the harbor frequently because of the unstable political situation in Nicaragua, the consul had far less time for writing than in his first post.

In spite of these drawbacks, Johnson quickly imposed order on the consulate and was able to return to New York, where he married Grace Nail on 10 February 1910. He had met Grace in her parents' Brooklyn home while he was living in New York. During his years abroad they had corresponded, and he had visited her during a leave from his Venezuelan post in 1907. Between leaving his consulate in Venezuela and taking up his new post in Nicaragua, he visited New York again in 1909, and the two had become engaged. Soon after the wedding Johnson had to hurry back to Corinto, for a revolution that had begun in Nicaragua the previous fall was growing more serious. Although Grace had been reared in a wealthy home and must have found even the remodeled consulate primitive, she adapted cheerfully to her new environment. For Johnson, Grace's presence made Corinto a happier place.

Through 1912 he continued to press for a better post. He favored duty in France, remembering both his happy times in that country on his trip with Rosamond and Cole years before and the lost chance to go to Nice. Negotiations were upset, however, with the election of Woodrow Wilson. Secretary of State William Jennings Bryan was determined to see that Democrats were rewarded for their loyalty, and, in spite of earlier assurances about the merit system governing consuls, the best Johnson could hope for would be to remain in Nicaragua for the next four to eight years. Having published *The Autobiography of An Ex-Colored Man* early in 1912, though anonymously, and having seen his poem "Fifty Years" appear in the *New York Times,* Johnson reluctantly resigned from government service in September

1913, perhaps feeling that he could support himself and Grace by his writing if necessary. To symbolize the change he was making, Johnson changed his middle name from William to the more literary-sounding Weldon.

The *New York Age*

By the fall of his first year as a free-lance writer, Johnson welcomed the opportunity to join the staff of the *New York Age* as contributing editor. Although the job did not pay a living wage, it supplemented his earnings as a songwriter and allowed him to keep his name before the public and to express himself on racial matters. He would maintain his connection with the *Age* for nearly nine years, from 15 October 1914, to 14 July 1923. One of his first editorials for the *Age* might have come from the *Daily American*. Of the role of Negro weeklies such as the *Age,* Johnson said, "They are organs of propaganda. Their chief business is to stimulate thought among Negroes about the things that vitally concern them."[9]

And Johnson did stimulate thought in the editorials that followed. Looking at the positive side of black life in New York, he pointed to the Harlem branch of the public library as a resource for learning: "I suppose if we were denied admission to this institution we would be hammering for entrance—as it is, we are admitted on the same terms as all other persons and we fail to take full advantage of our opportunity" (5 November 1914). Johnson suggested that his readers could give themselves a liberal education by setting up a course of reading in the library. As in his early days as a Florida journalist, he was quick to point out the shortcomings of the race; for example, in an editorial entitled "Rowdyism" he deplored the reputation Harlem was acquiring and protested, "We don't want Harlem to become known as a bad section simply because fifty or a hundred colored men and boys think that to be 'tough' is something smart" (23 September 1915).

Often Johnson took up the subject of black leaders. In "Responsibilities and Opportunities of the Colored Ministry" he stressed the power of the black church and urged that it become "not only the instrument for promoting our spiritual welfare, but our welfare as men and citizens" (8 February 1917). He singled out black leaders as diverse as Booker T. Washington and Marcus Garvey for comment, saying in an obituary column that Washington would be "an inspiration for many generations to come" (18 November 1915), and lamenting the failure of Garvey's Black Star line as "a disaster to the Negro" (30 June 1923), though he stopped short of defending Garvey, who had just been convicted of mail fraud.

White bigotry and unfair laws were frequent targets of Johnson's column. In December 1914 he attacked the Supreme Court, which had failed to rule against the enforcement of Jim Crow laws on trains, and in "The Importance of the Negro to the South" he pointed out an irony in southern attitudes toward the Negro. The South, he noted, had always considered the Negro a burden economically, but with the advent of labor recruiters from the North, laws were being passed to make recruiting a crime. "Perhaps this threatened exodus will bring a fuller recognition of the great importance of the Negro to the South," he closed (31 August 1916).

World War I was the occasion for a series of columns. In "Shall the Negro Fight?" Johnson concluded that "the Negro should never cease to claim the rights of American citizenship, and also that he should never shirk the duties of American citizenship" (15 February 1917). This stand did not keep him from attacking the manner in which black soldiers and sailors were used, however. As war preparations proceeded, he reacted to recruiting posters circulated through the South calling for enlistments by white men "experienced in the handling of colored men" to serve as noncommissioned officers in the army. Johnson asked, "Does the War Department have any idea of what it means in the South to have experience handling Negroes? It generally means to have the qualifications of a slave driver, of a chain-gang guard, of an overseer of the roughest kind of labor. . . . If it is decreed that white men must officer colored regiments, then at least let them be Northern white men who have no 'experience' " (8 November 1917). He also deplored the role black sailors played in the navy, noting that "from the earliest times down to within recent years, colored men have been able seamen, and gunners in the navy. Now, colored men are not wanted in the navy except as servants. Some action should be taken at once to remedy this condition" (29 November 1917).

As contributing editor of the *Age,* Johnson remained interested in poetry, founding a "Poetry Corner" in 1915 and inviting contributions. Although he occasionally printed his own poetry, he generally published the work of new poets and reviewed the work of others. As he saw it, the encouragement of art was closely allied to his work for civil rights and the improvement of his race, for "the world does not know that a race is great until that race produces great literature. . . . No race that produced a good literature has ever been looked upon by the world as distinctly inferior" (7 September 1918). Much of the work on *The Book of American Negro Poetry* grew out of Johnson's involvement with the *Age* Poetry Corner, and an article, "Aframerican Poets" (24 March 1923), drew heavily on his introduction to that anthology.

The NAACP

Neither Johnson's newspaper work nor his songwriting kept him from accepting the position of field secretary for the NAACP when it was offered in December 1916. His task as field secretary was by no means easy. In addition to organizing branches in various cities, most of them in the South, Johnson investigated lynchings and race riots throughout the United States, frequently at considerable risk. In 1920 he was elected secretary of the NAACP, the first black in that office, which he held until 1930. In spite of his heavy workload with the NAACP, he stayed with the *Age* during his entire tenure as field secretary and for the first few years as secretary.

Johnson's wide range of experience in many different areas gave him a breadth of vision unparalleled among the black writers of his day. Among other products of that vision would be books of poetry, collections of the creative work of others, a history, and an inspirational autobiography. The first book-length work to appear, however, was his controversial novel with the deceptive name, written mostly while Johnson was at his post in Venezuela. Although it was his only novel, *The Autobiography of an Ex-Colored Man* would eventually become one of the most influential Afro-American books of its time.

Chapter Two
The Autobiography of an Ex-Colored Man

Before he left New York to take up his diplomatic duties in Corinto, Johnson had written two chapters of a novel and submitted them to Brander Matthews, his former English professor at Columbia, who encouraged him to develop the book. Once in Corinto, Johnson had time to devote to the novel, and composition of the first draft went smoothly although he was not to publish the book until 1912. Nearly stillborn when it was first issued by Sherman, French, & Company in Boston, *The Autobiography of an Ex-Colored Man* became one of Johnson's chief claims to fame as a creative writer after it was reissued by Alfred A. Knopf during the height of the Harlem Renaissance.

Passing for White

Johnson's only novel, first published anonymously as "a human document" (*A,* 238), purports to be the autobiography of a light-skinned Negro who has elected to pass for white after a long struggle to make the most of his role as a black man in the United States. Born the illegitimate son of a quadroon servant and a wealthy white southerner, the nameless protagonist moves with his mother from Georgia to Connecticut after his father becomes engaged to the daughter of "another great Southern family."[1] He grows up without realizing his racial identity until an ugly incident at school identifies him as "colored." Following this revelation, he alternately feels shame at being identified with an "inferior" race and proudly resolves to excel in his chosen field, music, so as to become a great man and disprove the stereotype that denigrates him.

After his mother's death, he travels south to enroll in Atlanta University, but when his money is stolen, he abandons that plan and drifts through a number of occupations—cigar-roller in Jacksonville, Florida, professional gambler and ragtime musician in New York City, and finally paid companion of a mysterious white millionaire

20

who takes him to France, England, and Germany. While on the Continent, he rediscovers his old ambition of becoming a superior black man and returns to the United States to collect southern black folk music and to compose music inspired by the songs he has collected.

As he travels through the South collecting music, he shrinks from the poverty and social ostracism that are the lot of rural southern black people. He is finally deflected from his mission when he witnesses the lynching of a black man. Leaving the South immediately, he goes to New York, where he changes his name and appearance and enrolls in a business college. His business education enables him to obtain a good job; he saves his money, invests in tenement houses, and amasses a small fortune.

A moral crisis arises when he falls in love with an attractive white woman. Following a considerable struggle, he tells her about his racial background, and after overcoming her own reservations, she marries him. By the time his wife dies, they have two children, who know nothing of their mixed heritage. At the end of the novel the protagonist reflects that in a sense he has been "a coward, a deserter" (210), and he longs to be able to rejoin his mother's race. While he observes the strides being made by Booker T. Washington and other pioneers of his race, he feels "small and selfish," realizing that he has chosen the easy way out and has settled for becoming "an ordinary successful white man who has made a little money" (211) when he might have been one of the architects of a new role for black Americans.

Sources of *The Autobiography*

So convincing is Johnson's first-person narrative that its audiences, from the early reviewers to present-day readers, have always found it difficult not to identify the protagonist with his creator. Yet Johnson was drawing not on personal experience but on his imagination and on the experiences of a longtime friend. He also used two different prototypes as background for the creation of the ex-colored man's millionaire patron.

Throughout *Along This Way* Johnson frequently mentions a Jacksonville friend, whom he refers to only as D——. Eugene Levy, in his 1973 biography of Johnson, states that D—— is Judson Douglass Wetmore, and notes that Johnson never publicly identified D——, who had crossed the color line and passed for white.[2] Johnson first met

Wetmore in Jacksonville when both were about eight years old, and the two boys became best friends even though they were "unlike each other in more ways than one" (A, 33). A major point of difference was complexion: while Johnson's brown skin and features distinctly identified him as a Negro, Wetmore was to all appearances white. Because of conflict with his father, Wetmore ran away from home just before entering Atlanta University and went to New York. He shared a room with Johnson during Johnson's first year at the Atlanta preparatory school; he was "extremely good-looking, having, in fact, a sort of Byronic beauty. . . . Neither in color, features, nor hair could one detect that he had a single drop of Negro blood" (A, 76).

Unlike the ex-colored man, Wetmore completed his course of studies at Atlanta University, but after graduation he used a small legacy from his mother to travel around the country, living well among "Negro sporting circles" until his money was gone and most of his possessions were in pawnshops. After that he returned to Florida. As a boy he had learned to roll cigars in his father's cigar factory; now he lived in Tampa as a cigar maker until Johnson persuaded him to return to Jacksonville, where he joined Johnson in the publication of the *Daily American.*

When the newspaper failed, Wetmore did some electioneering for a local banker running for Congress, and was rewarded by having his expenses paid for a year at the University of Michigan. While Wetmore was at Michigan, a strange thing happened to him. All his life he had lived as a Negro, but at the university he failed to advertise his race and was assumed to be white. When he realized what had happened, he simply accepted the situation and spent the academic year of 1897–1898 living as a white man.[3] At the end of his year at Michigan, Wetmore returned to Jacksonville, studied law with Johnson's help, passed the bar examination, and joined Johnson in practicing law. Although Johnson does not go into detail in *Along This Way,* it seems probable that, during their close association at this time, Wetmore told him stories about his adventures while passing for white.

The law partnership broke up when Johnson moved to New York to write music with Rosamond. In 1905 Wetmore, who had prospered as a Jacksonville lawyer, left his practice there and bought into the practice of a black attorney in Brooklyn. Eventually Wetmore set up a practice of his own, and Johnson noted on visits to his office that most of his clients were white. Wetmore married a Jewish girl who knew that he was technically "colored," but whose family did not know. Like Johnson's fictional character, Wetmore had taken the step that would cut him off from the black race.

Although Johnson specified that a prototype for the eccentric millionaire in his novel was an unnamed friend of Al Johns, a black songwriter whom Johnson knew during his New York days, it seems likely that the character also owes much to the white doctor, T. O. Summers, for whom Johnson had worked in Jacksonville in 1888–1889. Like the millionaire patron of the ex-colored man, Summers appeared to have everything to live for but eventually took his own life. Even during the Jacksonville years Summers had given Johnson the feeling that he nursed some secret melancholy, perhaps because he would frequently sit "inhaling from a small can of ether, seemingly lost in dreams" (*A*, 95).

Finally, though he never passed for white, Johnson was able to use many of his own experiences as material for the book. The settings of the novel—Atlanta, Jacksonville, the New York tenderloin, and even Europe—were places that he knew firsthand. The prayer meetings and rural cabins that the ex-colored man visits in search of material were a part of Johnson's life during his summers as a teacher in rural Georgia. The experiences of the protagonist with Jim Crow laws before he makes the decision to pass were based upon deeply felt events in Johnson's own life. Even the lynching that convinces the ex-colored man to pass for white might have had its origin in the incident when Johnson was apprehended by the National Guard after the Jacksonville fire.

Composition

Judging by the condition of the original autograph manuscript, composition of *The Autobiography of an Ex-Colored Man* seems to have gone smoothly. Most changes from first manuscript to final printed novel are minor differences in punctuation, paragraphing, and diction. However, in a few places Johnson did make substantial alterations. Perhaps the most significant omission from the autograph manuscript concerns the lynching. In manuscript, the rumors that precede the lynching deal specifically with rape and murder, while in the published version of the novel the reader must infer the nature of the crime. The ending of the novel in the manuscript was both more compressed and more positive than in the published version: the protagonist's wife was alive, they had two children, and they were reasonably happy.

The typescript of the novel introduces several changes that emphasize social issues: a lengthy addition to chapter 10 elaborates on the theme of shade prejudice within the black race during the discussion of Washington's black society; in that same chapter a Civil War veteran is given a few more lines in his argument with a bigoted Texan; and an ironic allusion to "the great white throne" in heaven is inserted into the account of the southern camp meeting. Less significant additions appear at the end of chapter 4, where details of the ride in the Pullman porter's closet are added at the typescript stage, and in chapter 9, where two paragraphs are added to the description of British customs and language.[4]

In spite of the apparent ease with which Johnson wrote his only novel, the book would eventually have great impact and serve as a seminal work for two very different branches of Afro-American writers: those exposing specific social problems in the black community and those using black life to illuminate the general human condition. *The Autobiography of an Ex-Colored Man* is not only a cogent analysis of social conditions between black and white Americans at the turn of the century but the ironic portrait of a man who searches for, but never finds, his true identity.

Social Implications of *The Autobiography*

From the first, Johnson's book was considered valuable for the light it shed on race relations in the United States. Reviewing the novel for the *Crisis,* Jessie Fauset mentioned that it covered nearly every phase of the American racial scene, from North to South,[5] while fifty years later the respected black critic Sterling A. Brown judged the novel to be important because it was "the first to deal with Negro life on several levels, from the folk to the sophisticated," and added that *The Autobiography* is "rather more a chart of Negro life than a novel."[6] Certainly one of Johnson's purposes in writing the book was to depict the lot of the black American and to comment upon it, and his plot, which takes the protagonist from South to North and back again, from America to Europe and back again, allows Johnson ample scope for his observations and comments.

Before he realizes his own racial identity, Johnson's protagonist observes the effects of race in a quiet northern small town. A black boy whom he calls "Shiny" is the most intelligent pupil in the class, yet "in spite of his standing as a scholar, he was in some way looked down upon" (14). Soon after making this observation, the narrator sees another black child attacked by his classmates on the way home from school. If, as Johnson suggests elsewhere, prejudice must be learned, children begin to absorb the lessons at an early age. Years later, on an ocean crossing, the ex-colored man witnesses the same type of discrimination against a black doctor, the intellectual and moral superior of most of the people who object to sharing a table with him. Unlike "Shiny," however, the black doctor is willing to challenge attempts to segregate him.

When he leaves his small town after the death of his mother, the ex-colored man is exposed to more serious evidence of the inferior opportunities allotted to black people. On the train to Atlanta he meets a young Pullman porter who is a college student working to pay for his education. The porter, having learned the facts that his naive friend is only beginning to comprehend, tries to show him how a "colored" man lives in the South. He takes him to a shabby rooming house where railroad men sleep in shifts on the unmade beds. The protagonist's reaction to the lower-class residents of his new neighborhood is that of a fastidious white man: "The unkempt appearance, the shambling, slouching gait and loud talk and laughter of these people aroused in me a feeling of almost repulsion" (55–56). Later, while visiting Washington, D.C., with a friendly black doctor, the ex-colored man gives silent assent to the latter's judgment that black loafers standing on street corners represent the race to whites, while it should be represented by "the best it has been able to produce, not by the worst" (156). If he is repelled by the neighborhood, he is nauseated by the restaurant to which his new friend takes him. The room is smoky and filled with sickening odors; the floor is covered with sawdust and the tables with oilcloth; the silverware and dishes need to be washed. When he asks the porter why they are eating at such an inferior restaurant, he is told that this is the best "colored" restaurant in Atlanta. Later, in the New York black bohemia, the ex-colored man will discover that, although the accommodations are better than in the South, they are still aimed almost exclusively at the black trade and are usually less comfortable than those allotted to whites.

But Johnson's main character has gone to the South to learn about his black heritage, and not all that he learns is negative. When he reaches Jacksonville, he enters polite black society for the first time and finds that the highest class of southern black society has a rigidly governed code of conduct that determines who shall be admitted to its card parties, dances, and literary discussions. At a ball he attends while working as a cigar maker and piano teacher, he first sees a cakewalk, the dignity and stateliness of which so impress him that he declares the cakewalk one of the four main contributions of the Negro to American culture, the other three being the Uncle Remus stories, the Jubilee songs, and ragtime music. Later in the book he feels equal racial pride in the dramatic preaching and group singing at "big meetings" in rural southern churches.

In New York he encounters ragtime music again and elaborates on its importance as a contribution, but at the same time he notes one of the injustices of the music business: because the black creators of ragtime songs are often natural musicians who play by ear, their songs may be stolen by white men who record these improvisations and publish the songs under their own names, thus earning a great deal, while the black originators of the songs work for a few dollars a night. The other criticism the narrator expresses about the reception of ragtime, which he soon learns to play, is that conservative American musicians feel great contempt for the new music. Perhaps because of its black origins, ragtime is either ignored or dismissed as a temporary fad, less worthy than the imitative music produced by traditionally educated musicians.

Discrimination is appparent to the ex-colored man on the stage as well. He notices that one black minstrel singer does impressive readings from Shakespeare during impromptu entertainments in a black club, although in his professional roles he "was a man who made people laugh at the size of his mouth" (105–6). He also notes that among the white slummers who visit the club for sexual or psychological reasons, there is a group of white actors who play "darky" roles in blackface. These actors imitate the speech and actions of the black entertainers and are paid far more than their black models can ever hope to earn.

But it is violence, not mere discrimination, that finally leads the protagonist to pass for white. A hint of the white bigot's potential for violence is given during an argument between a liberal and a conservative on the racial question when the latter states that "anything—no country at all—is better than having niggers over you" (160). This man is clearly ready to fight the Civil War all over again if necessary. In reality, however, violence is usually limited to individual incidents, such as the lynching that causes the ex-colored man to forsake his mother's race.

The lynching surprises both the protagonist and the reader. Earlier, while traveling as a white man in Europe, the ex-colored man had been embarrassed when a Frenchman asked whether it was true that a black man had been burned to death in the United States. While he has previously been intellectually aware of such incidents, the ex-colored man must now confront the experience in person. Following a successful period of collecting black music throughout the South, he attends a "big meeting" that features two gifted southern preachers. He spends the night at the home of a black teacher. That night, he hears the sounds of voices and of galloping horses in the streets of the small Georgia town and takes advantage of his apparent whiteness to go outside and investigate. He finds that the Negro perpetrator of some "terrible crime" is being sought. He later witnesses the arrival of the fugitive and is unable to force himself to leave when the crowd chains the man to a post. Then "fuel was brought from everywhere, oil, the torch; the flames . . . leaped up as high as their victim's head. He squirmed, he writhed, strained at his chains, then gave out cries and groans that I shall always hear. The cries and groans were choked off by the fire and smoke; but his eyes, bulging from their sockets, rolled from side to side, appealing in vain for help. Some of the crowd yelled and cheered, others seemed appalled at what they had done, and there were those who turned away sickened at the sight" (187). Unable to turn away, Johnson's protagonist is riveted to the spot until long after the burning is over. It is the most effective propaganda scene in Johnson's novel.

In addition to his direct observations, the protagonist of *The Autobiography of an Ex-Colored Man* frequently interrupts his narration with extended analytical passages in which he comments upon the racial policies and customs of the nation. It is undoubtedly these passages more than any other facet of the novel that have caused many critics to treat the book less as a novel than as a fictionalized commentary, one in which Johnson's main character is merely a mouthpiece through which he can utter his own opinions. But *The Autobiography of an Ex-Colored Man* is a novel, and the analytical passages, like everything else, must be viewed as a part of the fiction even though they contain a great deal of truth.

Soon after he discovers that he is classified as black by his community, the narrator finds that all of his thoughts, words, and deeds are influenced by the notion of race. He realizes that it is hard for white people to know what black people really think. Because the Negro must never forget his unique racial role, he may find it impossible to be frank with whites and may unburd en himself completely only "in the freemasonry of his own race" (21–22). Many Negroes at the turn of the century find it best to hide their true natures "under cover of broad grins and minstrel antics" (22). On the other hand, because whites belong to the dominant culture, they have no need to dissemble. They show their true natures, and so "the coloured people of this country know and understand the white people better than the white people know and understand them" (22).

But behind his mask, the Negro is strengthened by the freemasonry of the race and continues a quiet struggle against oppression. His resistance is normally passive; he "bears the fury of the storm as does the willow-tree" (75), but he forces the white society of the South to employ most of its energy just to keep him in his place. Yet the South has lost two battles already and now faces a third: "The battle was first waged over the right of the Negro to be classed as a human being with a soul; later, as to whether he had sufficient intellect to master even the rudiments of learning; and today it is being fought out over his social recognition" (75).

Every phase of the campaign is not as hopeful as this statement would indicate, however. The white world has managed to infect black society with some of its pernicious notions. This influence is most apparent in the existence of a "peculiar inconsistency" within the black race regarding skin color. In Washington, D.C., the ex-colored man observes that "black men generally marry women fairer than themselves; while, on the other hand, the dark women of stronger mental endowment are very often married to light-complexioned men. . ." (154). The result, as he notes, is that the most successful stratum of the race is becoming lighter. But this is no inconsistency on the part of the Negro, the narrator concludes. He is simply following the rule spelled out to him by the dominant white society, particularly in the South: "Have a white skin, and all things else may be added unto you" (155).

In another sociological passage in *The Autobiography* Johnson explains through his narrator how the white South divides black people into three classes—the "desperate class," servants, and "independent workmen and tradesmen"—and treats each group differently. The desperate class is made up of ex-convicts and other members of a semicriminal element who "cherish a sullen hatred for all white men, and . . . value life as cheap" (77). Although this class is numerically small, its high visibility does a great deal to foster ill will between the races. The whites of the South realize that this class is dangerous to their own well-being, but instead of attacking the social ills that have given birth to it, they attempt to control it "just about as a man would a vicious mule, a thing to be worked, driven, and beaten, and killed for kicking" (77–78). The violence used against this class breeds more violence and drives a wedge between the two races.

The remaining two groups are viewed paradoxically. The servant class occupies the opposite end of the spectrum from the desperate class. Its members, from washerwomen to waiters, are viewed by the whites with indulgent tolerance and provide their white employers with some insight into the workings of the black mind, although these insights are limited by the mask behind which all black people must hide their true emotions. The self-employed tradesmen and artisans, unlike the servants, occupy a place in society as distant from the whites as that of the desperate class. Money or education usually results in a raised standard of living that places a gulf between the rising black family and its white neighbors. The ex-colored man makes this clear through an example: an upper-class white woman would be likely to attend her black cook if the latter were ill, but if the cook's educated daughter, having married a black businessman, "were at death's door," the lady would be prevented by custom from setting foot inside her house to help her (79).

Such distinctions are wiped out, however, when the black southerner of whatever class boards a train. There all classes are relegated by law to the Jim Crow cars. Through his narrator, Johnson is quick to point out that the highest class of black people does not really want to ride with white people or to escape riding with lower-class blacks. The problem is that the Jim Crow cars are inferior accommodations for which black passengers pay full fare.

On his travels through the South the ex-colored man avoids the Jim Crow cars because he is naturally taken for white even without making an effort to pass. On one trip he goes to the smoking car and overhears a debate on race that Johnson sets up in nearly the form of a morality play. The participants are a Jewish businessman, a college professor, an elderly veteran of the Union army, and a Texas cotton planter. When the "Negro question" arises, both the businessman and the professor artfully straddle the issue. The Jew, as a member of another minority group, is unable to sanction the oppression of black people, but he fears to oppose it because of his own uncertain status. The college professor, originally from the North, acknowledges having had liberal views before seeing conditions in the South, but now admits that southern whites are handling the racial situation well. The Civil War veteran humiliates the professor by suggesting—accurately—that he fears the loss of his job if he speaks out against bigotry. The real debate is waged between the veteran and the Texan. In spite of revealing some prejudices of his own—he refers to black people as "niggers"—the old soldier stands firm on the grounds of equal rights for all Americans. He debunks the Texan's claims for the superiority of the "Anglo-Saxon" race by asking him what "great fundamental and original intellectual achievements . . . may be credited to the Anglo-Saxon" (162) and by pointing out that if the Negro is as inferior as he is said to be, it should be unnecessary to enforce his position with the maze of laws and taboos that dominate the South. The Texan can only answer that no logical argument can sway him from his beliefs. The fact that the debate ends, not with hard feelings, but with a good laugh and a shared drink from the Texan's pocket flask suggests that, for even the most liberal white man, the question of the rights of the Negro is an intellectual rather than a highly charged emotional issue.

The picaresque nature of Johnson's novel provided him with excellent opportunities to incorporate social criticism of life in various parts of the United States, but perhaps even more important than the social issues the book raises are the psychological questions about the way the black race views itself.

The Ironic Layer of *The Autobiography*

On the first page of *The Autobiography* Johnson establishes the tone of the novel and suggests the complexity of the narrator. The ex-colored man begins by analyzing his motives for revealing "the great secret of [his] life"; while he feels a perverse sort of pride in his accomplishment, he also has a "savage and diabolical desire to gather up all the little tragedies of [his] life, and turn them into a practical joke on society" (3). However, the second paragraph suggests that the account is to be read not only as a boast, but also as a confession; the narrator admits, "And, too, I suffer a vague feeling of unsatisfaction, of regret, of almost remorse, from which I am seeking relief, and of which I shall speak in the last paragraph of this account" (3). The reader who turns to the end of the book at this point finds the key to one of the central ironies of the novel: the practical joke may, after all, be on the narrator, who laments "a vanished dream, a dead ambition, a sacrificed talent" and struggles to free himself of the fear that he has "chosen the lesser part" or sold his "birthright for a mess of pottage" (211). The narrator's first paragraph gives the reader the impression of a self-assured man with a rather objective, analytical approach to what promises to be a searching and honest account of his life. However, the second and last paragraphs alert the reader to the fact that the narrator-protagonist is in reality disturbed, torn by doubt; therefore, his statements should be examined carefully to determine the psychological facts concealed by superficial meanings. The unreliable nature of the narrator is thus suggested, and the reader who keeps this in mind will appreciate *The Autobiography* as a novel rather than as a guidebook to Negro life, as an account of emotional and psychological responses rather than as a mere history of the protagonist's social and financial rise in the world.

The main character's relationship with his father and mother, treated mainly in chapters 1 through 3, illustrates Johnson's ironic use of the unreliable narrator. An examination of what the narrator tells us suggests that he harbors an unrealized resentment toward both of his parents. The father, in particular, is treated harshly although he is not overtly criticized for his treatment of the narrator and his mother. The narrator's earliest memories of his father center not on traits of character or physique, but on the material objects associated with him: shiny boots or shoes, a gold watch and chain, the slippers his small son must bring him, and the coins doled out as presents. When the father is about to send his mistress and son north so that his white fiancée won't learn about them, he drills a hole in a gold piece and ties it around his son's neck. The narrator wryly comments, "More than once I have wished that some other way had been found of attaching it to me besides putting a hole through it" (6). This flawed gold piece serves as a fitting symbol for most gifts the white man has given the black as well as for the white man's materialistic values, values which the protagonist later adopts as his own. The father's action evokes suggestions of the bonds of slavery, and his choice of a going-away present is another example of his substitution of material gifts for overt recognition. Another suggestion of a master-slave relationship occurs later when the father comes to visit: he addresses his son as "boy" and the son responds, "Yes, sir" (34). Thus, the reader is prepared to recognize the irony in the mother's statement to her son that his father is "a great man, a fine gentleman" who loves them both very much (38); moreover, there is a sort of double-edged irony in her assertion that "the best blood of the South" is in her son (18). The relationship between father and son is epitomized in one incident: the father sends his son a new upright piano; however, the boy wonders why the gift wasn't a grand piano. Clearly, although the narrator tells of his father's kindness and his own emotional indifference in purely objective terms, the suggestiveness of the illustrative details and the psychologically revealing nature of apparently casual remarks make the reader aware of the protagonist's true feelings—resentment toward the father and his strictly materialistic expressions of affection.

While the narrator states that he loves his mother very much, there is evidence that Johnson attempted to convey more ambivalent feelings, the negative aspects of which are primarily subconscious. The mother's closeness to her son, her loving embraces, her desire to see him well educated—these are balanced by less admirable characteristics. She does not tell her son that he is partly black until he has been ridiculed as a "nigger" by schoolmates, and she hides the reality of his illegitimacy from him as long as possible. Even such minor details as the mother's practice of scrubbing him "until [his] skin ached" (4), as if to make him even more white than he is, suggest that she accepts the white world's value system, and thus helps to create the confused marginal being that her son becomes. The incident that is most indicative of the son's subconscious feelings about his mother occurs when, after several years, the father first visits them in the North. The mother is obviously delighted, but the son, awkward and embarrassed, soon rushes off to a musical rehearsal where he is to accompany a white violinist, a girl with whom he is infatuated. Although he is under no great pressure to invent an alibi for being late, he tells his teacher that his mother is seriously ill, near death. Subconsciously then, the narrator reveals his feelings: jealousy of the love his mother has for his father and, possibly, resentment of her black race that has so lowered his position in the eyes of his classmates and of himself. The wish-fulfillment element in the lie is not admitted by the narrator even when his mother really does die shortly thereafter; he attributes his pang of guilt to having prophesied her death. The protagonist's professed great love for his mother is an important factor in his attempt to accept his black identity, just as his hidden resentment of her "tainted blood" is one of the underlying factors in his ultimate rejection of the black race.

Johnson's most notable irony is reserved for the narrator's comments about himself. It is significant that passages that deal with his reactions and feelings are characterized by a neoromantic style, by sentimental and rather inflated diction. The narrator views himself in romantic terms, as a tragic hero whose flaw is the black blood he has inherited from his beloved mother. However, the reader, responding to the irony that undercuts the romantic pose, is more likely to view him as an antiheroic or pathetic character, frequently indulging in self-pity and unable to accept his total identity and assume his position in a race for which he feels little sympathy or admiration. Indeed, at times the reader suspects that the main character may have the makings of a first-class bigot in his own personality. Because the narrator's view of himself is distorted and because his narrative is, in a sense, an attempt to justify his decisions, the reader must question everything the main character says about himself.

The narrator strikes many ironic notes in telling about his boyhood. One of his minor but meaningful memories is his preference for the black keys on the piano. This choice would seem to suggest that the protagonist feels that "black is beautiful," that he is subconsciously drawn to his mother's race even before he is aware of his mixed parentage. However, closely juxtaposed to this memory is an account of how some black classmates were mistreated:

Sometimes on the way home from school a crowd would walk behind them repeating:

> "Nigger, nigger, never die,
> Black face and shiny eye."

On one such afternoon one of the black boys turned suddenly on his tormentors and hurled a slate; it struck one of the white boys in the mouth, cutting a slight gash in his lip. At sight of the blood the boy who had thrown the slate ran, and his companions quickly followed. We ran after them pelting them with stones until they separated in several directions. I was very much wrought up over the affair, and went home and told my mother how one of the "niggers" had struck a boy with a slate. I shall never forget how she turned on me. "Don't you ever use that word again," she said, "and don't you ever bother the coloured children at school. You ought to be ashamed of yourself." (14–15)

It is, ironically, only a short time after his participation in this attack that the main character is shocked to find himself classified with these pariahs when the principal of his school divides the class into white and colored. The protagonist is surprised by the reactions of the two races: the black children in the class, some of whom he has persecuted, say that they have known his secret all along but would not unmask him; however, his former friends jeer, "you're a nigger too" (16). This experience and the realization that his mother belongs to the black race make the narrator determined to consider himself black and to live his life accordingly. This is the first of several courses chosen by the protagonist, who vacillates between opposing bigotry in society and learning to live within the system, until his final capitulation.

Even before his humiliating discovery, the main character has admired the leading scholar of their class. Without meaning harm, he has tagged the black classmate with the nickname "Shiny," an obvious pun on the racial slur, "shine." After he realizes that he is identified with the black children, he feels an even closer tie with Shiny. At their graduation ceremony Shiny's well-delivered oration profoundly moves the protagonist: "the effect upon me of 'Shiny's' speech was double; I not only shared the enthusiasm of his audience, but he imparted to me some of his own enthusiasm. I felt leap within me pride that I was coloured; and I began to form wild dreams of bringing glory and honour to the Negro race. For days I could talk of nothing else with my mother except my ambitions to be a great man, a great coloured man, to reflect credit on the race and gain fame for myself" (45–46).

However, the same incident illuminates the other side of the protagonist, for he also speculates on the enthusiastic reaction of the largely white audience. Instead of accepting this response as a matter of course, the narrator admires the whites' willingness to overlook race when a performance is sufficiently superior. He believes that "the explanation . . . lies in what is a basic, though often dormant, principle of the Anglo-Saxon heart, love of fair play" (45). It is ironic that elsewhere the narrator holds these same white parents accountable for the cruel bigotry their children exhibit toward the black students.

From time to time throughout the novel, when the narrator interrupts the movement of the story to generalize about Negro life and experience, the reader can hardly help being struck by the objective tone of his observations. After he knows he is a Negro, he comments: "And this is the dwarfing, warping, distorting influence which operates upon each and every coloured man in the United States. He is forced to take his outlook on all things, not from the view-point of a citizen, or a man, or even a human being, but from the view-point of a *coloured* man. It is wonderful to me that the race has progressed so broadly as it has, since most of its thought and all of its activity must run through the narrow neck of this one funnel" (21).

Although the protagonist has apparently accepted his membership in the race he is describing, his attitude toward black people is curiously aloof. In the next section of the novel, chapters 4 through 10, the main character's experiences provide him with opportunities to observe many facets of Negro life, but he consistently views that life as an outsider might and constantly reverts to white values, attitudes, and responses. (The fact that the narrator's observations of black life in America have been so highly praised by readers and critics adds an element of irony that Johnson may not have foreseen.)

After his mother's death the main character decided to attend Atlanta University, for the South holds a "peculiar fascination" for him; it is there, he feels, that he must work out his destiny and start toward his goal of becoming "a great coloured man." However, there is an ironic gap between his expectations and the reality he finds in Atlanta. When the Pullman porter takes him to the boardinghouse, the protagonist's first response to the race that he has decided to join verges on repulsion: "Here I caught my first sight of coloured people in large numbers. I had seen little squads around the railroad stations on my way south, but here I saw a street crowded with them. They filled the shops and thronged the sidewalks and lined the curb. I asked my companion if all the coloured people in Atlanta lived in this street. He said they did not and assured me that the ones I saw were of the lower class. I felt relieved, in spite of the size of the lower class" (55). His stomach turns when he is taken to a greasy basement restaurant, and the culmination of his disillusionment occurs when all his plans are thwarted because his money is stolen, ironically by the very porter who has served as his guide.

Unable to enter the university or to find work in Atlanta, the narrator travels to Jacksonville. Perhaps because Jacksonville is smaller than Atlanta and presented a less harsh aspect in the late nineteenth century, the main character is not so confused or appalled and is able to think about what he sees there. Once again adopting that clinical

tone so characteristic of his comments on the black race, he analyzes
the three socioeconomic classes of black people already discussed. Objective analyses like this one, which occupies eight pages in the 1927
edition, have encouraged the sociological approach to the novel, but
such digressions also tell us something about the narrator. He is able
to view "his" race in detached sociological terms because he never
feels a part of it. He never succeeds in his attempts to find his identity within the race to which the country's laws and customs consign
him, the race that he embraced because it was his mother's. This ability to step outside the race is a reminder of the ironic gap between
his true character and the flattering self-portrait the narrator draws of
a man earnestly attempting to do what he knows is right. However,
beneath his air of detachment the reader is allowed to glimpse an individual whose racial identity changes because he bases his life on unstable principles. The protagonist's vacillating principles as well as
his changing "color" were emphasized, in fact, by Johnson's alternate
title for the novel, *The Chameleon.*[7]

The protagonist experiences a different black culture in New York,
where he is introduced to the black gambling houses and the "sporting life." Still the sociological analyst, he notes a curious attitude
among white New Yorkers. Rather than isolate the Negro as do the
southerners, the New York upper classes enjoy slumming trips to
black places of amusement. Ironically, the fact that the narrator is
himself an observer of black life enables him to recognize and classify
the motives of the slummers:

There was at the place almost every night one or two parties of white people,
men and women, who were out sight-seeing, or slumming. They generally
came in cabs; some of them would stay only for a few minutes, while others
sometimes stayed until morning. There was also another set of white people
who came frequently; it was made up of variety performers and others who
delineated "darky characters"; they came to get their imitations first-hand
from the Negro entertainers they saw there.

There was still another set of white patrons, composed of women; these
were not occasional visitors, but five or six of them were regular
habituées. . . . I always saw these women in company with coloured men.
They were all good-looking and well dressed, and seemed to be women of
some education. (107–8)

Due to the prudish literary conventions of 1912 Johnson's narrator is
not very explicit about black-white sexual relationships, but his reac-

tion to the sight of one woman with her black gigolo is revealing: "I shall never forget how hard it was for me to get over my feelings of surprise, perhaps more than surprise, at seeing her with her black companion; somehow I never exactly enjoyed the sight" (109). Not even the constrained understatement can conceal the fact that his reaction is that of a white man.

The narrator's ability as a ragtime pianist attracts the attention of the New York millionaire who becomes his patron and offers to take him to Europe. The narrator seems oblivious to the unintentional irony in the millionaire's invitation: " 'I think I'll take you along instead of Walter.' Walter was his valet" (124). In a way, the millionaire replaces the father in the master-servant relationship that seems to characterize the protagonist's experiences with white men. While the narrator states with pride that his patron treats him "as an equal, not as a servant" (130), we also learn that the millionaire "fell into a habit which caused me no little annoyance; sometimes he would come in during the early hours of the morning and, finding me in bed asleep, would wake me up and ask me to play something" (131). Johnson uses the European trip to throw certain characteristics of American racial attitudes into relief, but the trip also takes the protagonist away from the difficulties of the life he has tried to lead. Accepted as a white man in Europe, he again dreams of becoming a great colored man and plans to go back into "the very heart of the South, to live among the people, and drink in my inspiration firsthand. I gloated over the immense amount of material I had to work with, not only modern rag-time, but also the old slave songs—material which no one had yet touched" (142–43). The irony of his exploiting the music of the Negro escapes him.

On his way to the South he encounters two men whose racial attitudes impress him. The first of these is a black doctor whom he meets on the ship. A member of what W. E. B. DuBois called the "talented tenth," the doctor is described by the narrator as "the broadest-minded coloured man I have ever talked with on the Negro question" (151). The narrator seems unaware that his high opinion of the doctor is determined by the many similarities between the man and himself. Like the protagonist, the doctor can discuss the "Negro question" in objective, detached terms. Only when his personal freedom is threatened does the doctor become emotionally involved enough to resent racial prejudice; on being informed that a man has attempted to have him evicted from the dining room, the doctor responds: "I don't object to anyone's having prejudices so long as those prejudices don't interfere with my personal liberty. Now, the man you are speaking of had a perfect right to change his seat if I in any way interfered with his appetite or his digestion. . . . but when his prejudice attempts to move *me* one foot, one inch, out of the place where I am comfortably located, then I object" (150). Also like the protagonist, the doctor deplores the fact that some classes of black people are not so culti- vated as he, and in some ways he can sympathize with southern atti- tudes. When the two men visit some of the doctor's friends in Boston, the narrator's comments are significant: "I could not help be- ing struck by the great difference between them and the same class of coloured people in the South. In speech and thought they were genuine Yankees. The difference was especially noticeable in their speech. There was none of that heavy-tongued enunciation which characterizes even the best-educated coloured people of the South. It is remarkable, after all, what an adaptable creature the Negro is" (152–53). Thus, even in the midst of his resolve to become a great black man, the narrator feels shame for all but the most acculturated of his race; his standards are white standards and may cause the reader to recall the millionaire's observation, "My boy, you are by blood, by appearance, by education, and by tastes a white man" (144).

The second important encounter occurs in the smoking car. As the narrator listens to the Texan defending his extreme anti-Negro posi- tion against the Civil War veteran, he feels most sympathetic toward the racist Texan: "I must confess that underneath it all I felt a certain sort of admiration for the man who could not be swayed from what he held as his principles" (165). The total absence of any emotional response to the Texan's slurs is another indication of the fact that the main character doesn't feel like a member of the insulted race. In spite of all his experiences, his psychological orientation has not changed since he was a boy, joining the whites who chased the "nig- gers" home from school.

The burning to which the main character attributes his decision to pass for white is indeed traumatic; the narrator's reaction is notable for two reasons: he seems to feel no pity for the victim, yet for him- self he feels humiliation and shame. Just as in previous comments on Negroes, the narrator is distant and unsympathetic in describing the man being burned: "There he stood, a man only in form and stature, every sign of degeneracy stamped upon his countenance. His eyes were dull and vacant, indicating not a single ray of thought" (186–

87). However, the effect the scene has on him is intensely emotional: "I walked a short distance away and sat down in order to clear my dazed mind. A great wave of humiliation and shame swept over me. Shame that I belonged to a race that could be so dealt with; and shame for my country, that it, the great example of democracy to the world, should be the only civilized, if not the only state on earth, where a human being would be burned alive" (187–88). While the reader probably sympathizes with the shame the character feels for his country, he undoubtedly wonders at the man's lack of hostility toward the white Americans who are burning the Negro. The narrator goes on to justify to himself the decision he has made:

I argued that to forsake one's race to better one's condition was no less worthy an action than to forsake one's country for the same purpose. I finally made up my mind that I would neither disclaim the black race nor claim the white race; but that I would change my name, raise a moustache, and let the world take me for what it would; that it was not necessary for me to go about with a label of inferiority pasted across my forehead. All the while I understood that it was not discouragement or fear or search for a larger field of action and opportunity that was driving me out of the Negro race. I knew that it was shame, unbearable shame. Shame at being identified with a people that could with impunity be treated worse than animals (190–91).

Significantly, the narrator maintains the fiction that he is not taking a positive step toward choosing the white race, but he must know the result of letting "the world take [him] for what it would." Thus, he takes the step toward which he has unconsciously been moving from the beginning, but there is bitter irony in the fact that the narrator chooses to ally himself with the persecutors rather than the persecuted, to be one of those who can, without shame or remorse, treat other human beings as animals.

As he has certainly foreseen, everyone who meets him assumes that he is white, and he rises quickly, both socially and financially. For a time, he enjoys the sensation of playing a practical joke on white society, and thinks how surprised his new acquaintances would be if he revealed his true identity. However, the joke recoils on him when he falls in love. While he is agonizing over whether he should reveal his secret, he and the girl encounter "Shiny," who, in contrast with the main character, has made a distinct effort to help black people by teaching in a black southern college. Emboldened by his loved one's friendly response to Shiny, the main character tells her the truth about himself, only to feel himself "growing black and thick-featured and crimp-haired" (204). She bursts into tears, and the narrator sums up his own feelings by confessing, "This was the only time in my life that I ever felt absolute regret at being coloured, that I cursed the drops of African blood in my veins and wished that I were really white" (205). This statement, as the reader has had ample opportunity to see, is false. From the time he was first called "nigger" by his schoolmates, the main character has fought against being classified as a Negro. However, it is only at this point that he acknowledges the revulsion against his black blood, his inheritance from his beloved mother.

Eventually, the girl accepts the protagonist as he is (something he has never been able to do himself) and marries him. They live happily until she dies after bearing him two children. Near the end of the novel the narrator at last faces his life honestly: "Sometimes it seems to me that I have never really been a Negro, that I have been only a privileged spectator of their inner life; at other times I feel that I have been a coward, a deserter, and I am possessed by a strange longing for my mother's people" (210). An address by Booker T. Washington causes the ex-colored man to reflect again and to feel "small and selfish" compared to those who "are publicly fighting the cause of their race" (211). Ironically, in spite of his efforts to ignore the advice of his millionaire friend, he has followed it—"make yourself as happy as possible" (146). However, the happiness of being a successful white man now seems insufficient recompense for his unfulfilled dreams of contributing to Negro musical achievement. Self-realization has come at last, if only reluctantly and tentatively, and the ex-colored man fears that he has been the real victim of the practical joke he has played on society. The low-keyed ending of the novel is much more effective and realistic than the melodramatic conclusions so typical of earlier black novels on the "tragic mulatto" theme.

Johnson's achievement in *The Autobiography of an Ex-Colored Man* deserves recognition. The book has a significant place in black literature because it overthrows the stereotyped black character, employed even by early black writers, in favor of one that is complex and many-sided. Johnson gains depth and subtlety by using the first-person point of view rather than the third-person favored by his contemporaries. Moreover, Johnson's skill in using an unreliable narrator who reveals more than he intends—indeed, more than he knows—adds important psychological dimensions to the main character and his story. Finally, Johnson's skill in conveying his vision of black life in America by means of irony rather than the propagandistic techniques of his predecessors marks a new, more artistic dimension for the black novelist.

The Reception of *The Autobiography*

Although Johnson's novel attracted relatively little attention when it was published in 1912, it remained in print until 1918 as indicated by advertisements in the *Crisis* "Book Mart" advertisements. However, the 1927 Knopf edition, coming as it did at the height of the Harlem Renaissance and at a time when Johnson was perhaps the best-known member of the older generation of black writers, was considerably more influential. Handsomely printed and well distributed, this edition of the novel was reviewed widely not only in America but in England also. Critics from the 1930s to the present have always considered it one of the important novels of the early part of the century, and in 1965 it was reprinted, along with Booker T. Washington's *Up From Slavery* and W. E. B. DuBois's *The Souls of Black Folk*, as *Three Negro Classics*, edited by John Hope Franklin.

As important as the critical recognition the book has received is the implicit tribute of later creative writers, ranging from Jessie Fauset and Nella Larsen to Ralph Ellison and James Baldwin. More than the other novelists of his day—writers such as Charles W. Chesnutt, Sutton Griggs, Paul Laurence Dunbar, and W. E. B. DuBois—Johnson remains a lasting influence on the Afro-American novel as seen, for example, in the picaresque form of *Invisible Man* and its nameless narrator or in the self-hatred of Baldwin's John Grimes in *Go Tell It on the Mountain*. Although Johnson was never to write another novel, the book that he did produce has left an indelible imprint on the history of black American literature.

Chapter Three

Johnson's Poetry: The Two Voices

During his Atlanta years Johnson began to write poetry. From the 1890s through his publication of *Fifty Years and Other Poems* (1917) the form and subject matter of his poems are characteristic of the period in which he wrote; that is, they are written in conventional stanzaic forms, in rhymed verse, and they address subjects that are either the conventional subject matter of the poet or the specialized subject matter of the Afro-American poet, as handed down from early protest writers such as George Moses Horton and Frances Watkins Harper. During the 1920s, however, Johnson began to experiment with more modern forms, eventually producing in *God's Trombones* (1927) a free verse form calculated to recall the style and rhythm of the southern black minister. These later poems are the ones most likely to appear in literary histories, despite the popularity of some early poems such as "Lift Every Voice and Sing."

Finding a Voice

Characteristic of Johnson's early poetry is a Petrarchan sonnet, "Mother Night," that he wrote while serving as consul in Venezuela. The night is personified as "a brooding mother" out of which the universe evolved and to which it will return. In the sestet Johnson applies the lesson of the universe to the life of the individual:

> So when my feeble sun of life burns out,
>   And sounded is the hour for my long sleep,
>   I shall, full weary of the feverish light,
>   Welcome the darkness without fear or doubt,
>   And heavy-lidded, I shall softly creep
>   Into the quiet bosom of the Night.[1]

Another poem of the same type is the English sonnet called "Sleep" in *Fifty Years* and "Blessed Sleep" in *St. Peter Relates an Incident*. Reminiscent of Sir Philip Sidney's Sonnet 39 from *Astrophel and Stella*, "Sleep" praises the value of sleep, its ability to "soothe the torn and sorrow-laden breast." But near the end the poem diverges from Sidney's theme, reflecting on the fact that pain "lives again so soon as thou art fled." The final couplet moves on to another form of sleep: "Man, why should thought of death cause thee to weep; / Since death be but an endless, dreamless sleep?" (*FY*, 50). While he wrote several of these conventional poems, which display the sort of competence and deftness with rhyme and meter that made him a successful songwriter, Johnson would probably never have merited a place in literary history for any of this class of poetry. Even in his early period, however, he did write a number of poems whose racial themes gained them a place in Afro-American literary history. Certain of his occasional or commemorative poems are widely anthologized, while some protest poems produced between 1893 and 1917 deserve to be better known than they are.

The fiftieth anniversary of the Emancipation Proclamation was the occasion for "Fifty Years," the well-known title poem of his first volume of verse. Johnson begins his long poem by recalling how far the race has come, not only in the fifty years since Emancipation, but since its introduction to America three centuries earlier:

> A few black bondmen strewn along
> The borders of our eastern coast,
> Now grown a race, ten million strong,
> An upward, onward marching host.
> (*FY*, 2)

He asserts the rights of America's black citizens to equal partnership with white citizens because "this land is ours by right of toil," and he details the contributions of black men and women to clearing the land and making it productive. Johnson also points out that from the martyrdom of Crispus Attucks to his own day black Americans had rallied to the flag in times of war; he forcefully concludes this section, "We've bought a rightful sonship here, / And we have more than paid the price" (*FY*, 4). The black American, then, has no need to take a position inferior to that of the newly arrived European immigrant who, black leaders such as Booker T. Washington feared, might replace black workers in the desirable jobs in the industrialized North. On the other hand, "Fifty Years" acknowledges that black people are still persecuted and that many have grown discouraged. Johnson ends the poem, therefore, with an exhortation to the black reader to maintain his courage, to look beyond the present:

> That for which millions prayed and sighed,
> That for which tens of thousands fought,
> For which so many freely died,
> God cannot let it come to naught.
>
> (FY, 5)

"Fifty Years" appeared in the *New York Times* on 1 January 1913[2] and has been frequently anthologized since, but it is more noteworthy for the sentiments it expresses than for the excellence of the poetry itself. While at times genuine emotion breaks through its formality, the modern reader may be inclined to read it more as a social document than as a great poem.

Similar to "Fifty Years" is "Father, Father Abraham," written on the anniversary of Abraham Lincoln's birth and first published in the *Crisis* in February 1913. Johnson pays tribute to the Great Emancipator, a traditional hero of the race, in a prayerlike poem of sixteen lines. As the biblical Abraham gave birth to the Jewish people, Lincoln is viewed as the spiritual progenitor of the black race. Furthermore, Lincoln's death is seen as an act of martyrdom to "ransom" the black race. The poem not only offers a tribute to the statesman, but also contains an inspirational note:

> To-day we consecrate ourselves
> Anew in hand and heart and brain,
> To send this judgment down the years:
> The ransom was not paid in vain.
>
> (FY, 13)

Also in this category is "Lift Every Voice and Sing," a poem which Johnson's brother Rosamond set to music. Designed to be sung by a large chorus of school children, "Lift Every Voice" was first performed at a celebration of Lincoln's birthday in Jacksonville in 1900. In later years it was adopted by the NAACP and became known as the "Negro National Hymn" or the "Negro National Anthem." Like "Fifty Years," "Lift Every Voice" looks back to the hardships faced by the race in the past—"stony the road we trod, bitter the chastening rod"—and also looks forward to "the rising sun of our new day begun."[3] While he details some of the pains of slavery, Johnson's emphasis is on the moderate course: the race should learn from the "dark past," should persevere in its faith in God and the nation, and should never cease to press toward its eventual victory.

Less artificial and more moving than the public poems discussed above is Johnson's "O Black and Unknown Bards," a commemoration of the anonymous composers of the spirituals. In this justly popular poem Johnson allows his honest emotion to break through the conventional diction of turn-of-the-century popular verse and pays a beautiful tribute to the folk poets who produced the spirituals. He opens the poem by posing an unanswerable question:

> O black and unknown bards of long ago,
> How came your lips to touch the sacred fire?
> How, in your darkness, did you come to know
> The power and beauty of the minstrel's lyre?
> *(FY, 6)*

Throughout the poem he weaves lines from the actual spirituals—"Steal Away to Jesus," "Swing Low, Sweet Chariot," "Go Down, Moses," and others—marveling at the ingenuity of the composers, who produced their works without any training and under the worst possible conditions. And it is not merely as artistic successes that Johnson views the songs, but as signs of the spiritual depths of their creators. Himself an agnostic, Johnson nevertheless empathizes with the "hungry hearts" of the listeners for whom the songs were composed. Implicit in the poem is a recognition of the importance of religion in helping an enslaved people to survive with their spirits intact.

Like many black poets, Johnson frequently turned to the writing of protest poetry. At times the protest is mild, as in "O Southland," where his love for the South is mingled with his desire to see it progress toward racial harmony to the benefit of both races. More typically, however, his protest poems display a bitterness and a militancy that are surprising in the poetry of a man who normally took moderate stands on civil rights issues. The earliest published poem of this type, "A Brand," appeared in 1893 during Johnson's junior year at Atlanta University. The poet describes a despised wanderer:

> Upon his brow he wore a brand,
> And on his back,
> A thousand stripes for it he bore:
> His skin was black.[4]

Yet, at the end of a miserable life, the wanderer faces his God and is admitted to heaven because of his pure heart. Johnson progressed from the mild protest of "A Brand" to a warning in "To America" that the fate of the nation itself is tied to the fate of its black population. Hardly militant, "To America" states that if black people are kept "sinking 'neath the load we bear," the race will throw chains about the feet of their country instead of helping the nation to prosper (*FY*, 5).

Protest poems such as "Brothers" and "The White Witch" go a step further by addressing the twin southern problems of lynching and miscegenation. "Brothers" begins with words spoken by a member of the lynch mob, observing a victim "more like brute than man" and asking if this creature is from the same "docile, child-like, tender-hearted race" that has served southern whites for three centuries. The victim replies that he is "the bitter fruit . . . of planted seed" and details the "lessons in degradation, taught and learned," that have been the lot of the race through fifteen generations of slavery and oppression: the slaves separated from their families, the murders and the rapes he has seen. The poem then shifts from dramatic dialogue to detailed description of the lynching itself as the mob refuses to hear more accusations. The fire is built carefully so that it will not burn too fast and deprive the watchers of the joy of watching their victim die slowly. When it begins to burn too vigorously, they throw water on it. At last the black man dies, and the crowd comes forward for grisly souvenirs of the burning: "You take that bone, and you this tooth; the chain— / Let us divide its links; this skull, of course, / In fair division, to the leader comes." Finally, their brutal actions over, the members of the mob have time to ponder the last words of the dying man, but they fail to unlock the riddle. His words, in the last line of the poem, are "Brothers in spirit, brothers in deed are we" (*FY*, 14–17). Although much of the dialogue of this poem is artificially formal, given the heated context, the poem on the whole makes a powerful statement about violence and brutality begetting more brutality.

"The White Witch" is more subtle, though it is unlikely that any black reader would mistake its message.[5] "The White Witch" appears to be a fanciful supernatural ballad, in which a vampirelike witch threatens to lure away young men and kill them. Beneath the surface, however, it is clear that Johnson is treating black-white sexual relations, the complex of psychological ills that accompany the thought

of miscegenation, and the very real physical danger to the black man
who succumbs to the lures of white women. The white witch is described by one who speaks, perhaps from the grave, about his own
temptation and fall. He warns his younger brothers not to test their
strength against the witch or even to look at her, "For in her glance
there is a snare, / And in her smile there is a blight" (*FY*, 19). The
witch is not like the witches the boys have heard of in children's stories; this is no "ancient hag" with "snaggled tooth," but a beautiful
woman "in all the glowing charms of youth." The third and fourth
stanzas create a portrait of her as the archetypal white woman: "her
face [is] like new-born lilies fair," her eyes are blue, and her hair is
golden. Although she appears young, "unnumbered centuries are
hers" (*FY*, 19); her origins go back to the beginning of the universe.

The speaker then tells his brothers how he has been trapped by the
witch. At first he enjoyed the kisses from her unnaturally red lips and
the bondage of her white arms and the golden hair that entangled
him. But then a transformation took place, and the red lips began to
"burn and sear / My body like a living coal" (*FY*, 20). The temptress
has led her victim to the stake, and the glow of her beauty becomes
the glow of the lynch mob's fire. What motivates the white witch?
In anticipation of much later works such as Calvin C. Hernton's *Sex
and Racism in America* (1965) or Eldridge Cleaver's *Soul on Ice* (1968)
her victim answers:

> She feels the old Antaean strength
> In you, the great dynamic beat
> Of primal passions, and she sees
> In you the last besieged retreat
> Of love relentless, lusty, fierce,
> Love pain-ecstatic, cruel-sweet.
>
> (*FY*, 21)

The poem ends with the repeated warning to the younger brothers
not to be enticed by the witch. Johnson operates with considerable
subtlety in this poem. Nowhere is it stated that the speaker and his
brothers are black, but given the imagery of the white enticer and the
nature of the speaker's fate, it is apparent that the poem is a social
fable on one level even though it may be read on another.

Although Johnson's later experiments with free verse in *God's
Trombones* were extremely successful, he never completely abandoned
traditional verse. Just three years after the publication of *God's Trom-*

bones, a news story that caught Johnson's eye provided the occasion for another poem. As he tells the story in his foreword to *St. Peter Relates an Incident,* he read about a contingent of gold-star mothers being sent to France to visit their sons' graves. White mothers were to travel on one ship and black mothers on another, the latter being a "second-class vessel" (*SP,* ix). Johnson laid aside the manuscript that he had been working on and began to compose the long satirical title poem of his last collection of poetry.

In the 161 lines and six sections of "Saint Peter Relates an Incident of the Resurrection Day" Johnson uses various stanza forms, rhyme schemes, and meters, but most of the work is in quatrains made up of rhyming couplets. The first two sections set up the framework for the tale itself: to enliven the cloying sameness of heaven, St. Peter tells the assembled angels and saints a story. On the day of the resurrection all of the living and dead members of the various patriotic groups of the United States, including the Ku Klux Klan and Confederate veterans, gathered in Washington to honor the Unknown Soldier and escort him to heaven. Since the tomb of the Unknown Soldier is so massive, he could not emerge immediately, and the assembled masses had to dig him out. For his part, the Unknown Soldier worked from inside, until at last

> He, underneath the débris, heaved and hove
> Up toward the opening which they cleaved and clove;
> Through it, at last, his towering form loomed big and bigger—
> "Great God Almighty! Look!" they cried, "he is a nigger!"
>
> (*SP,* 18)

The crowd debated the best way to handle the situation. The Klan suggested reburying the soldier, but skeptics argued that divine will would not be foiled by mere concrete. While they were discussing him, the Unknown Soldier climbed to heaven, singing "Deep River." St. Peter recalls:

> I rushed to the gate and flung it wide,
> Singing, he entered with a loose, long stride;
> Singing and swinging up the golden street,
> The music married to the tramping of his feet.
>
> (*SP,* 20)

The poem ends with the heavenly perspective on the incident as the assembled host disperses while making a noise "that quivered / 'twixt tears and laughter" (*SP*, 22). Characters and incident, meter and rhymes—all contribute to the humorous effect of the poem.

In addition to the title poem, Johnson's last collection of poetry contains four other poems not included in *Fifty Years*, all but one of which revert to conventional verse forms. In his formal traditional poetry he breaks no new ground, but his poetry is competent, and, because of the unique racial perspective from which it approaches life, it is worth reading. One further contribution that Johnson made to black poetry of his period is a body of dialect verse.

The Dialect Poems

When Johnson began his poetic career in the 1890s, dialect poetry was in fashion. One well-known black poet of the period, Paul Laurence Dunbar, had been encouraged to create dialect verse by the influential novelist and critic, William Dean Howells. When Johnson moved to New York, the conventions demanded dialect in the songs and shows that he wrote for the stage. It is not surprising, then, that of the poems in *Fifty Years and Other Poems*, the last sixteen are grouped under the heading "Jingles & Croons," meaning dialect poems. As he read and edited poetry during the early twentieth century, however, Johnson began to have reservations about dialect in poetry; by the time he published his last collection of poetry, he had already experimented with an alternative to the stylized dialect he and Dunbar had earlier used, and he no longer believed that dialect was a proper part of the black poet's repertoire. Accordingly, *St. Peter Relates an Incident: Selected Poems* reprinted only eight of the sixteen dialect poems that had appeared in *Fifty Years*. Furthermore, Johnson prefaced these poems with a two-page statement of his later position on dialect poetry.

By the middle of the 1930s, Johnson says, dialect poetry as it was known in the latter half of the nineteenth century and the early years of the twentieth was a dead form, never used by black writers. If black poets of the thirties used dialect at all, it was "the racy, living speech of the Negro in certain phases of contemporary life." Modern black poets, including Johnson, had left behind the "smooth-worn stereotype" of "contented, childlike, happy-go-lucky, humorous, or forlorn 'darkies' with their banjos, their singing and dancing, their watermelons and possums . . ." (*SP*, 69). He regrets the tainted origins of conventional black dialect, which came to the black poet via the white minstrel show and the plantation tradition, for that dialect could be used powerfully, as when it was used by folk poets who were composing unselfconsciously, "solely to express and please themselves" (*SP,* 69). Had black poets "been the first to use and develop the dialect as a written form, . . . to work it in its virgin state, they would, without doubt, have created a medium of great flexibility and range, a medium comparable to what Burns made of the Scottish dialect" (*SP,* 70). But the form came to the black poet too heavily freighted with old associations and conventions, and he was never able to break it free from its past. The future, Johnson predicts, would have to see a new idiom evolve to capture the spontaneity and "racial flavor" that dialect poets attempted to convey.

Johnson had been hesitant about including any of his own dialect poems in his last collection, but he reflects that some great poems had been written in dialect: "To take Dunbar's dialect poetry out of American literature would cause both a racial and a national loss" (*SP,* 70). The same might be said of some of Johnson's dialect poems, such as "Sence You Went Away," which has often passed for a genuine folk poem, and even "Brer Rabbit, You's de Cutes' of 'Em All," which is indebted to the plantation tradition.

"Sence You Went Away" laments a lost love. The speaker finds all of nature wanting now that his loved one has left him:

> Seems lak to me de stars don't shine so bright,
> Seems lak to me de sun done loss his light,
> Seems lak to me der's nothin' goin' right,
>   Sence you went away.
>
>   (*FY,* 63)

Although Johnson employs the sort of conventional dialect Dunbar used, "Sence You Went Away" is restrained in its tone and contains none of the malaprops that cause some dialect poems to belittle the speaker. The persona created by the speaking voice is dignified in his grief, and, dialect aside, the poem speaks to and for anyone who has lost a lover.

Another sort of tenderness is captured in "De Little Pickaninny's Gone to Sleep," which Johnson published in *Fifty Years* but omitted in the final volume of his poetry. The speaker is a worried father who fears that something is wrong with his child:

> Cuddle down, ma honey, in yo' bed,
> Go to sleep an' res' yo' little head,

> Been a-kind o' ailin' all de day?
> Didn't have no sperit fu' to play?
> Never min'; to-morrer, w'en you wek,
> Daddy's gwine to ride you on his bek,
> 'Roun' an' roun' de cabin flo' so fas'—
> Der! He's closed his little eyes at las'.
>
> (*FY*, 83)

But the father's relief gives way to uneasiness as the child sighs and groans in his sleep, and when the father goes to the trundle bed to reassure himself, he finds that the child has died. Johnson may have omitted the poem from his final book believing that it was too sentimental, but the sorrow expressed by the poem is understated:

> W'at's dat far-off light dat's in his eyes?
> Dat's a light dey's borrow'd f'om de skies;
> Fol' his little han's across his breas',
> Let de little pickaninny res'.
>
> (*FY*, 83)

The rest that the father had wished for his child has become the eternal rest.

More typical of dialect poetry from the turn of the century is "Tunk," a dramatic monologue based on Johnson's conception of one of his students in the rural Georgia school. The speaker is an angry mother who has tried to do the best thing for her son Tunk, only to have him refuse to cooperate in his education:

> Heah I'm tryin' hard to raise you as a credit to dis race,
> An' you tryin' heap much harder fu' to come up in disgrace.
>
> Dese de days w'en men don't git up to de top by hooks an' crooks;
> Tell you now, dey's got to git der standin' on a pile o' books.
>
> (*FY*, 66–67)

Tunk's mother warns him that a "darkey" has to work hard from first light in the morning to sundown, never earning more than he needs to stay alive, and never owning more than his clothes. On the other hand, she naively sees the lives of white workers as ideal. Not only do they work a much shorter day, but their work seems easy:

> Dey jes does a little writin'; does dat by some easy means;
> Gals jes set an' play piannah on dem printin' press machines.

Chile, dem men knows how to figgah, how to use dat little pen,
An' dey knows dat blue-back spellah f'om beginnin' to de en'.
(FY, 67–68)

While the moral of the poem, that black youth needs education to be
upwardly mobile, is unassailable, the portrait of the mother that
emerges from her speech is unflattering. She attempts to motivate
Tunk for the wrong reasons, seeing education as a license to practice
a life of idleness. Her naiveté about the lives of white people and her
acceptance of the term "darkey" for her race suggest a condescension
on the poet's part that was far from Johnson's true attitude. Yet, as
Dunbar's rise proves, such an image of the southern Negro fit white
America's stereotypes, as conditioned by the plantation school, and
Johnson was not immune to the effects of the stereotypes and conventions that he found established in dialect poetry when he began to
write it.

No such social questions arise to spoil the enjoyment of another
class of Johnson dialect poems—works like "Possum Song" and "Brer
Rabbit, You's De Cutes' of 'Em All." The first of these is a comic
warning to "Brudder Possum" that fall is coming and with it hunting
season. The second, a more complex poem, praises not only the physical "cuteness" of the traditional black trickster figure, but also the
acute instinct for survival that made Brer Rabbit a folk hero since the
days of slavery. The creatures of the wilderness have a meeting to determine "Who is de bigges' man?" An owl is appointed judge and
renders his decision in an oracular formula:

"Brer Wolf am mighty cunnin',
Brer Fox am mighty sly,
Brer Terrapin an' 'Possum—kinder small;
Brer Lion's mighty vicious,
Brer B'ar he's sorter 'spicious,
Brer Rabbit, you's de cutes' of 'em all."
(FY, 81)

When each of these animals except Brer Rabbit claims to have won
the competition, the wily rabbit "jes' stood aside an' urged 'em on to
fight" until all of the other animals were exhausted, then "he jes'
grabbed de prize an' flew" (FY, 82), proving that he was the "cutest"
in more than one sense.

While Johnson's achievements in traditional rhymed verse and in dialect poetry are not remarkable, he was among the foremost black poets of his day. If his work seems dated, so does much of the work of his famous contemporary Dunbar. But Johnson lived longer than Dunbar, lived to observe the experimentation in poetry that occurred during his lifetime and to modify his own writing accordingly.

God's Trombones

Johnson's greatest contribution to Afro-American poetry was nearly ten years in the making. In 1918, while lecturing in Kansas City, he was invited to speak at a black church, where he was to follow a visiting minister who had a considerable reputation as a preacher. It was late in the evening, and the prepared sermon began prosaically, but when he sensed that the attention of the congregation was wandering, the visiting preacher

stepped out from behind the pulpit and began to preach. He started intoning the old folk-sermon that begins with the creation of the world and ends with Judgment Day. He was at once a changed man, free, at ease and masterful. The change in the congregation was instantaneous. . . . It was in a moment alive and quivering; and all the while the preacher held it in the palm of his hand. . . . He strode the pulpit up and down in what was actually a very rhythmic dance, and he brought into play the full gamut of his wonderful voice, a voice—what shall I say?—not of an organ or a trumpet, but rather of a trombone, the instrument possessing above all others the power to express the wide and varied range of emotions encompassed by the human voice. . . . Before he had finished I took a slip of paper and somewhat surreptitiously jotted down some ideas for the first poem [of *God's Trombones*], "The Creation."[6]

Published in the *Freeman* in 1920, that first poem elicited favorable responses and was reprinted in several anthologies. However, the press of his work with the NAACP was so great that, in spite of some false starts on new free-verse poems, it was seven years before Johnson completed a second poem for *God's Trombones*, "Go Down Death."[7]

The book published in 1927 consists of seven free-verse sermons introduced by a preface in which Johnson explained the origin of the poems and the language in which they were written; he added a prayer, also in free verse, such as might have been offered in a real congregation before the sermon. He considered and discarded the notion of writing *God's Trombones* in dialect, he says in his preface, first because dialect verse is "a quite limited instrument. . . . with but two complete stops, pathos and humor" (*GT*, 7). Second, when they were preaching, the black preachers the poems attempt to capture did not really use black dialect but an elevated form of language, "a fusion of Negro idioms with Bible English" (*GT*, 9), and it is this language that Johnson set down in his verse sermons. In *Along this Way* he explained his use of free verse by saying that he chose "a loose rhythmic instead of a strict metric form, because it . . . could accommodate itself to the movement, the abandon, the changes of tempo, and the characteristic syncopations of his material" (*A*, 336).

"Listen, Lord," the opening prayer, gives a sort of preview of what is to come in the sermons. The inspiration that is called down upon the minister is couched in earthy, figurative language:

> Hang him up and drain him dry of sin.
> Pin his ear to the wisdom-post,
> And make his words sledge hammers of truth—
> Beating on the iron heart of sin.
> ....
> Put his eye to the telescope of eternity,
> And let him look upon the paper walls of time.
> Lord, turpentine his imagination.
> Put perpetual motion in his arms, ...
>
> (*GT*, 14)

Because of the unexpected nature of some of these images, they strike the reader with a force that recalls Edward Taylor's use of metaphysical conceits—such as "Who in this bowling alley bowled the sun?"— to approach religious subjects. Such language does not cause the reader to find an intellectually inferior speaker ridiculous but makes him admire the daring and strength of the basic metaphors.

This technique continues into "The Creation," although the diction of the first sermon is elevated appropriately above that of "Listen, Lord." God's motivation for the creation is human, basic, and understandable: "I'm lonely— / I'll make me a world" (*GT*, 17). The actual mechanics of creation are treated in detail chosen to form a mental picture of real activity in the mind of the listener:

> Then God reached out and took the light in his hands,
> And God rolled the light around in his hands

> Until he made the sun;
> And he set that sun a-blazing in the heavens.
> And the light that was left from making the sun
> God gathered it up in a shining ball
> And flung it against the darkness,
> Spangling the night with the moon and stars.
>
> (*GT,* 17–18)

One can easily imagine a preacher miming such actions. In the creation of Man a specifically black image is created.

> This Great God,
> Like a mammy bending over her baby,
> Kneeled down in the dust
> Toiling over a lump of clay
> Till he shaped it in his own image;
>
> Then into it he blew the breath of life,
> And man became a living soul.
>
> (*GT,* 20)

The anthropomorphic God who appears in these lines is maintained consistently throughout the poem. He is not the remote, formal, all-knowing God of the Scriptures so much as an approachable, questioning, evolving Being with whom the listener could identify. Creation is an act of problem-solving, as God seeks to remedy the loneliness that has plagued Him; thus He is not only an understanding but an understandable Being. The use of long and short lines suggests the changing tempo of the preacher's speech, and the occasional dashes indicate "a certain sort of pause that is marked by a quick intaking and an audible expulsion of the breath. . ." (*GT,* 10–11). On the whole, "The Creation" is a dignified poem whose tone and diction are appropriate to its solemn subject.

In later sermons, where the object is to sway the emotions of the congregation and to foster repentance, Johnson's preacher becomes more earthy and his idiom more colloquial, as in the second, fourth, and seventh sermons: "The Prodigal Son," "Noah Built the Ark," and "The Judgment Day." In "The Prodigal Son," after the famous opening of "Your arm's too short to box with God," the preacher immediately makes clear the central analogy of the parable:

A certain man had two sons.
Jesus didn't give this man a name,
But his name is God Almighty.
And Jesus didn't call these sons by name,
But ev'ry young man,
Ev'rywhere,
Is one of these two sons.

                                                    (*GT,* 21)

The preacher paints a rather specific picture of the prodigal son's de-
bauchery, detailing the charms of

. . . the women of Babylon!
Dressed in yellow and purple and scarlet,
Loaded with rings and earrings and bracelets,
Their lips like a honeycomb dripping with honey,
Perfumed and sweet-smelling like a jasmine flower. . . .

                                                    (*GT,* 24)

But he reminds his congregation that, like the prodigal son, each
man must someday face the end of riotous living. "But some o' these
days, some o' these days, / You'll have a hand-to-hand struggle with
bony Death, / And Death is bound to win" (*GT,* 25). This grim
metaphor leads him to the obvious conclusion: like the prodigal son,
his listeners will do well to mend their ways and return to their Father before it is too late.

   "Noah Built the Ark" and "The Judgment Day" are similar warn-
ings. The former sermon traces the origins of sin back to the Garden
of Eden and then on to Noah's time, lightening the sermon with an
occasional touch of humor: when Noah warns of the deluge to come,
"Some smart young fellow said: This old man's / Got water on the
brain" (*GT,* 35). The preacher leaves the moral of his tale to God,
who "hung out his rainbow cross the sky" and warned that the next
time He will "rain down fire" on mankind (*GT,* 37). This same image of fire raining down is the beginning of the final sermon of the
book, "Judgment Day." Here no humor relieves the solemn des-
criptions: the graves yielding up their dead to the sound of "the
clicking together of the dry bones" (*GT,* 54), the division of the sheep
from the goats, and the casting of the damned into hell. The poem,
as well as the volume, ends on this somber note: "Sinner, oh,

sinner, / Where will you stand / In that great day when God's a-going to rain down fire?" (*GT*, 56). Thus, in nearly half of the verse sermons Johnson emphasizes the fire-and-brimstone messages delivered by the old-time preachers.

But the sermons in *God's Trombones* can comfort the flock as well as threaten it with reminders of God's wrath. "Go Down Death—A Funeral Sermon" offers consolation to the "heart-broken husband," the "grief-stricken son," and the "left-lonesome daughter" of a woman who has died. The preacher dramatizes God's reaction when, looking down into the world, He sees "Sister Caroline, / Tossing on her bed of pain" (*GT*, 27) and orders Death to report to Him. Death is described in terms that are not so much fearful as majestic: his horse's hooves strike sparks from the golden streets of Paradise as he rides to the throne of God, and he leaves a trail like that of a comet in the sky as he embarks on his mission. Though the arms that he puts around Sister Caroline are cold, they soothe the pain she has felt, and Death looks "like a welcome friend" (*GT*, 29). Receiving the dead woman into heaven, Jesus

> . . . smoothed the furrows from her face,
> And the angels sang a little song,
> And Jesus rocked her in his arms,
> And kept a-saying: Take your rest. . . .
> (*GT*, 30)

If Death is not the mother of beauty, at least it is a welcome sleep after a lifetime of pain, a concept with which black congregations of the 1920s and even Johnson's more sophisticated black readers could empathize.

Although "The Crucifixion" also ultimately treats the salvation of mankind in its last lines, most of the poem deals in heartrending detail with the passion and death of Christ. At first there is no attempt to relate the sufferings of the Savior to those of the black people of the United States—sufferings of which Johnson was all too aware after his years of service with the NAACP—but a black congregation hearing such a sermon, like the black reader, would not need to be reminded of the parallel. However, after the preacher has taken his listeners through the mental anguish of Gethsemane and on through the trial, he incorporates the black folk belief about the race of Simon of Cyrene as Jesus carries the cross up to Golgotha:

I see my drooping Jesus sink.
And then they laid hold on Simon,
Black Simon, yes, black Simon;
They put the cross on Simon,
And Simon bore the cross.

(GT, 41)

Now the connection has become explicit, and, along with Jesus, the black listener could shudder at the sound of the hammer and feel the pain being inflicted.

The preacher reaches his high point in the poem as he dwells on the agony of Christ during the crucifixion; the repetition of key words and the alternate pattern of the lines relates this section of the poem to traditional litanies.

Jesus, my lamb-like Jesus,
Shivering as the nails go through his hands;
Jesus, my lamb-like Jesus,
Shivering as the nails go through his feet.
Jesus, my darling Jesus,
Groaning as the Roman spear plunged in his side;
Jesus, my darling Jesus,
Groaning as the blood came spurting from his wound.
Oh, look how they done my Jesus.

(GT, 42)

The end of the poem again separates the identities of listener or reader from that of the martyred Jesus as the preacher reminds his congregation, echoing the words of a familiar spiritual, how awesome was the sacrifice that redeemed them:

It causes me to tremble, tremble,
When I think how Jesus died;
Died on the steeps of Calvary,
How Jesus died for sinners,
Sinners like you and me.

(GT, 43)

Yet Jesus the scapegoat is also "King Jesus" in the poem, and "The Crucifixion" implicitly reminds its audiences—the fictional listener and the real reader—that the downtrodden do not remain down forever. A transfiguration awaits Jesus and may await His most humble follower.

"Let My People Go" also appeals to the black audience through identification of black people with the enslaved children of Israel in Exodus. Here Johnson draws on a traditional association between the two peoples of which, as a collector of spirituals, he was well aware. But the sermon "Let My People Go" depends little on the song of the same name, merely sharing a few lines with it. The preacher begins his account of Moses with the prophet's first encounter with God in the burning bush. The preacher's God soon shows Himself to be a Being of plain speech:

> And God said to Moses:
> I've seen the awful suffering
> Of my people down in Egypt.
> I've watched their hard oppressors,
> Their overseers and drivers;
> The groans of my people have filled my ears
> And I can't stand it no longer;
> So I'm come down to deliver them. . . .
> (*GT,* 46)

The terminology is that of slavery—overseers and drivers as opposed to the term "taskmasters" in the King James Bible—and God's double negative marks Him as having proletarian sympathies. He then delivers his order to Moses in nearly the same words as in the spiritual: "tell Old Pharoah / To let my people go" (*GT,* 46). The preacher relates the plagues and the death of the Egyptian firstborn that led to the release of the children of Israel, but he reserves his greatest power for the end of his sermon. In great detail he tells of the mighty army called up by Pharoah to pursue the fleeing slaves, picturing for his congregation the multitude of chariots raising dust "that darked the day" (*GT,* 51), and emphasizing the earthly power assembled against God's chosen people.

But all this power is useless when Pharoah and his hordes attempt to cross the Red Sea:

> Old Pharoah got about half way cross,
> And God unlashed the waters,
> And the waves rushed back together,
> And Pharaoh and all his army got lost,
> And all his host got drownded.
> (*GT,* 52)

The broader implications of the biblical story are clear when the preacher warns metaphorical "sons of Pharaoh" that they can never hold the people of God, a meaningful message to black people of the 1920s, who had been subjected to mistreatment ranging from discrimination to lynching, and who had seen the widely publicized Dyer antilynching bill killed by the 67th Congress early in the decade. "Let My People Go" is in many ways the most powerful work in *God's Trombones;* treating as it does the theme of God's rescue of the enslaved and the downtrodden, the poem strikes an old and responsive note in black literature.

Responses to Johnson's Poetry

Johnson's first book of poetry was largely ignored by the literary establishment, perhaps understandably. When *Fifty Years* appeared under the imprint of the Cornhill Company of Boston, Johnson was relatively unknown, having produced, in addition to his anonymously published novel, only a little more than a dozen poems, some of which appeared in periodicals of very limited circulation. Nevertheless, William Stanley Braithwaite, the black critic and poet who reviewed *Fifty Years* for the *Boston Evening Transcript,* stated that Johnson had proved himself to be the heir to Dunbar's position as "the most important poet of the race,"[8] and even suggested that Johnson was superior to Dunbar intellectually. Brander Matthews, Johnson's teacher at Columbia, praised the poet in the introduction he wrote for the volume, singling out the title poem as an example of superior diction, imagination, and craftsmanship. Benjamin Brawley, reviewing the volume for the *Journal of Negro History,* especially liked "Mother Night," "O Black and Unknown Bards," "The White Witch," and "The Young Warrior."[9] While some half-dozen other periodicals noted the publication of *Fifty Years and Other Poems* from 1917 through 1919, these favorable opinions did not prevail in the marketplace—the book sold slowly—or in the critical opinions of others, for the book was ignored by most reviewers. This is not to say that Johnson had no reputation as a poet. The popularity of some of his works, especially the song "Lift Every Voice and Sing," gave him a sort of underground reputation among black people that is impossible to quantify. Maya Angelou tells, for example, of the pride she felt in 1940 when she and her classmates replied to the segregationist speech of a white politician by singing the "Negro National

Anthem" as an assertion of their dignity and their determination to endure.[10]

God's Trombones, on the other hand, was very well received by the literary press. Unlike *Fifty Years,* it was published by a major firm, Viking Press, and its author was by 1927 perhaps the most visible black American alive. In literature he had made a name for himself as a critic of poetry with his anthology, *The Book of American Negro Poetry* (1922), and as an expert on spirituals with his two collections published in 1925 and 1926. His novel *The Autobiography of an Ex-Colored Man* was republished under Johnson's name in the same year that *God's Trombones* came out.

However, the reception of *God's Trombones* was not just a response to the reputation of its author, but a recognition of the excellence and originality of the poetry itself. Harriet Monroe, reviewing *God's Trombones* for her journal *Poetry,* had some reservations about the success of individual poems but felt that, on the whole, readers "should be grateful for this book,"[11] while the anonymous critic for *Saturday Review of Literature* felt that no student of black literature could afford to miss the book. The *New York Times Book Review* praised *God's Trombones* for its "sensitivity, artistic judgment, and a sustained emotional beauty."[12] Thomas Munroe, in the *New York Herald Tribune Books,* found "The Creation" to be "almost Miltonic" although he felt that some of the other poems might have been helped by the inclusion of dialect.[13]

Among black critics, Johnson fared even better than in the mainstream publications. *Opportunity* not only published a favorable review by Joseph Auslander but also awarded Johnson its first prize in literature for 1928.[14] Poet Countee Cullen, writing for the *Bookman,* felt that the attempt to replace dialect was successful and called "The Creation" and "Go Down Death" magnificent.[15] W. E. B. DuBois agreed with Cullen about the success of Johnson's attempt to convey the black idiom through means other than conventional dialect and identified Johnson as a trailblazer in black poetry, while Alain Locke termed Johnson a major poet.[16] Of the black critics reviewing *God's Trombones,* the faintest praise came from satirist Wallace Thurman, who lumped Johnson with Dunbar in the category of important minor poets. Yet even Thurman had to acknowledge that the free-verse sermons were among the best poems written by black poets.[17]

Half a century after its publication *God's Trombones* is recognized as Johnson's best poetry, and its influence on later black poets has been widely noted. Eugene B. Redmond, in *Drumvoices,* calls *God's Trombones* "one of the most precious [volumes] in the annals of Afro-American writing" and sees Johnson as an influence on Margaret Walker, Langston Hughes, and Sterling Brown.[18] Arthur P. Davis recognizes Johnson as "a pioneer influence" and suggests that "because of its folk undergirding, *God's Trombones,* in all probability, will outlast the rest of Johnson's poetry."[19] Blyden Jackson and Louis D. Rubin, Jr., conclude that "it was Johnson, more than any other man, who opened the path [to the creation of a new black poetry], and the achievement that followed was in an important sense possible because of what he first demonstrated. The leading poets who came afterward—Toomer, Hughes, Tolson, Hayden, Brooks, LeRoi Jones—can truly be said to have followed along James Weldon Johnson's way."[20]

So Johnson, who had abandoned early poetic ambitions in order to work in the fields of politics, journalism, and race relations, returned to poetry at various times during his life, and with considerable success. While only a few of his early poems merit inclusion in a list of significant works of Afro-American literature, *God's Trombones* is clearly his crowning achievement as a poet and will be remembered for its influence on later poets as well as enjoyed for the freshness and beauty of its imagery and language.

Chapter Four
Editor and Critic

During the 1920s and 1930s Johnson achieved considerable prominence in the black literary world for a number of reasons. His column "Views and Reviews" in the *New York Age* had been running weekly since 1914, and in it he had frequently reviewed books and written on literary matters. He was the author of a thin volume of poetry, *Fifty Years and Other Poems,* had published poetry both in black publications such as the *Crisis* and mainstream journals such as *Century* and the *Independent,* and in 1927 produced his successful experiment in free verse, *God's Trombones.* His authorship of *The Autobiography of an Ex-Colored Man* was unacknowledged until 1927, but black literary circles had identified him as the probable author. Furthermore, his position as secretary of NAACP gave him a visibility not enjoyed by strictly literary figures such as Charles W. Chesnutt, William Stanley Braithwaite, or Claude McKay. Before the decade of the 1920s was more than half over, Johnson had further reinforced his position by publishing two important anthologies, a collection of modern black poetry and a cross section of spirituals. By the end of the decade he had added a second anthology of spirituals and had written several critical articles in which he not only defended the achievements of his race in the arts but also identified some of the unique problems faced by black artists—what he called "the dilemma of the Negro author."

Throughout his work as an editor and critic Johnson was motivated by a creed that he enunciated in an essay published in 1932. "The conception of the Negro as a creative force in America is new," he noted. "For generations he has been thought of as a beggar at the gate of the nation, waiting to be thrown the crumbs of civilization; as crude material to be shaped and molded; but it is equally true that he has helped to shape and mold America."[1] In the prefaces of his anthologies and in his critical essays Johnson stressed the artistic and cultural shaping exerted by the Negro artist on the dominant culture of the nation.

The Book of American Negro Poetry

When Johnson's anthology of black poetry was first published in 1922, the Harlem Renaissance was barely under way. *Shuffle Along* had become a hit show on Broadway the year before, and Claude McKay's *Harlem Shadows* was to appear just months after *The Book of American Negro Poetry*. *Opportunity*, the journal of the National Urban League which encouraged many younger writers to join the renaissance, was not yet founded. The other famous books of the Harlem Renaissance—Jean Toomer's *Cane* (1923), Countee Cullen's *Color* (1925), Alain Locke's *The New Negro* (1925), Langston Hughes's *The Weary Blues* (1926), and McKay's *Home to Harlem* (1928)—were still in the future.

Johnson's contribution to the Harlem Renaissance collected the work of thirty-one poets, beginning with Paul Laurence Dunbar and including W. E. B. DuBois, William Stanley Braithwaite, Fenton Johnson, Benjamin Brawley, Claude McKay, Georgia Douglas Johnson, Jessie Fauset, Anne Spencer, and Johnson himself. Although some of these figures, such as DuBois, Brawley, and Fauset, were chiefly known for their work in fields other than poetry, writers such as McKay, Fenton Johnson, and Georgia Douglas Johnson had published as many as three volumes of poetry each. Yet to most readers of *The Book of American Negro Poetry* only Dunbar's name was familiar. Much of the verse previously published by the contributors appeared, like Johnson's own *Fifty Years*, in thin volumes issued by obscure printers. *The Book of American Negro Poetry*, published by Harcourt, Brace and distributed aggressively, was widely reviewed and brought its poets a greater audience than most had previously enjoyed.

In spite of Johnson's own personal preferences—for racial moderation and for poems that deal directly with racial themes, and against dialect poetry—the contents of his anthology are eclectic. For example, the Dunbar selections range from dialect poems like "When de Co'n Pone's Hot" to raceless poems like "Ships That Pass in the Night." Claude McKay is represented not only by such romantic poems as "The Harlem Dancer" and "Harlem Shadows," but by such militant poems as "If We Must Die," "The Lynching," and "To the White Fiends." Although Johnson made some prudent political choices by including DuBois (editor of the *Crisis*), Braithwaite (a black Brahmin who edited annual anthologies of magazine verse), and Fauset (one-time literary editor of the *Crisis*), he was also generous to the younger generation of poets: Fenton Johnson, McKay, and in the second edition Langston Hughes, Countee Cullen, Arna Bontemps, and Gwendolyn Bennett. To represent his own work, Johnson printed not only older poems in standard English such as "The White Witch" and parts of "Fifty Years" but his dialect poem "Sence You Went Away" and, looking forward to *God's Trombones,* his more experimental poem "The Creation."

Perhaps as important as the poetic content of the anthology, however, is the preface with which Johnson introduces the poems. In a lengthy essay, which was praised by a number of contemporary reviewers, he outlines the raison d'être for the collection, sketches the history of Negro-American poetry from Phillis Wheatley to modern times, and discusses his own theories about the subject matter and execution of racial verse. "The final measure of the greatness of all peoples," Johnson asserts, "is the amount and standard of the literature and art they have produced. The world does not know that a people is great until that people produces great literature and art. No people that has produced great literature and art has ever been looked down upon by the world as distinctly inferior."[2] While he acknowledges that the American Negro has yet to demonstrate his "intellectual parity" by producing a substantial body of literature and art, Johnson feels that the capacity to do so has been amply demonstrated by a number of distinct contributions in diverse fields: the "Uncle Remus" folk tales, the spirituals, the cakewalk and allied dances, and ragtime music. Although the artistry of some of these productions might be challenged, Johnson believes them to be "the only things artistic that have yet sprung from American soil and been universally acknowledged as distinctive American products" (*BNP,* 10). By this he means that most mainstream American art has evolved from European models, and that the American Indians, though they have produced noteworthy art, have had little impact on American culture at large. On the other hand, ragtime music has had such an impact that "American music" has become synonymous with ragtime, and white composers have borrowed (or stolen) freely from their black predecessors.

Johnson admits that in the more formal arts black writers and artists have done less than might be expected, but he suggests that the reason for this failure is that "the Negro in the United States is consuming all of his intellectual energy in this grueling race-struggle" (*BNP,* 21), the same struggle that is sapping the strength of the white South. But to turn to poetry, Johnson asserts that there have been accomplishments by black American writers, substantiating his claim by citing some of the more significant black poets from the eighteenth century to the twentieth.

Johnson points out that Phillis Wheatley began her writing career at a time when America had no great poets. He compares her work with that of Anne Bradstreet and suggests that Wheatley, although she wrote under handicaps that Bradstreet, the wealthy daughter of a Bay Colony governor, did not have to face, produced poetry of comparable quality. His discussion of Wheatley is not unqualified praise. He wishes that she had written under the influence of the Romantic poets rather than that of Alexander Pope. He notes that most of her poems are occasional verses addressed to prominent people and concludes that she was "far from being a democrat" (*BNP*, 30). And finally, he suggests that if she had come in closer touch with realities during her short life, she might have produced poems with some meaningful discussion of slavery in them. Nevertheless, he closes his treatment of Wheatley by stating that she "merits more than America has accorded her" (*BNP*, 31).

The poets who come after Wheatley and before Dunbar are admittedly of lesser talent than these two major figures. Johnson briefly notes the poetry of Jupiter Hammon, a contemporary of Wheatley's, before moving on to George M. Horton and Frances E. Harper, both of whom address the issue of slavery, Horton in rather plaintive terms and Harper with a more militant voice, of which Johnson approves. Because of the paucity of biographical information and criticism on these writers at the time his anthology was compiled, Johnson may not have known the one major difference between Horton and Harper that would account for the difference in their tone: Horton was born a slave and Harper free. The constraints that operated on a slave who hoped to earn enough from his writing to buy his liberty would not have affected the daughter of freemen. Although Johnson appreciates the techniques of both writers less than those of Wheatley, he praises their attempts to come to grips with the major fact of their lives— the existence of slavery.

Alberry A. Whitman earns praise from Johnson not only for his commitment to the search for justice but for the grandeur of the concepts he chose. Johnson notes that Whitman's poems such as "Not a Man, and Yet a Man" and "The Rape of Florida" are major works, the former over five thousand lines and the latter nearly half that length. Although some later critics have faulted Whitman for his sometimes careless poetic technique, Johnson chooses several of the better passages of the two poems for quotation in keeping with his belief that the poets who fall between Wheatley and Dunbar should be evaluated "more in the light of what they attempted than of what they accomplished" (*BNP,* 26). If Johnson's belief suggests special pleading for these nineteenth-century poets, it should be remembered that those who did not suffer directly from slavery were still subject to restraints on their freedom that white Americans did not experience. However, no qualification is necessary in the case of the last poet Johnson discusses in his historical survey.

Paul Laurence Dunbar is advanced by Johnson as the first black poet to combine flawless technique with the mastery of his material. Johnson traces Dunbar's career from the nonracial poetry in standard English in *Oak and Ivy* (1892) through the dialect poetry that dominated his later work. He quotes Dunbar as having told him that he disliked dialect poetry and felt that it hampered his efforts to grow as a poet. Yet Johnson, in spite of his own reservations concerning dialect poetry, feels that Dunbar achieved a great deal as "the first to use it as a medium for the true interpretation of Negro character and psychology" (*BNP,* 35). He notes that Dunbar was a living contradiction of the popular assumption that any special ability in a Negro was due to his having white blood, for Dunbar was of pure Negro ancestry. In what he accomplished with the idiom of his race, Johnson says, Dunbar most closely resembles Robert Burns. He also stresses that, while most people remember only the dialect verse, Dunbar continued to write poetry in standard English.

Closing his historical survey of black poetry in the United States, Johnson digresses for a moment to consider other black poets of the western hemisphere: Plácido and Manzano of Cuba, Vieux and Durand of Haiti, and Machado de Assis of Brazil. Because racism is not the factor in Latin American and Caribbean countries that it is in the United States, Johnson suggests that the first world-class poet of African descent may well come from an American country other than the United States.

Johnson then looks ahead to the contents of the anthology he has assembled and points out how few modern poets write in Negro dialect. The problem with dialect, he contends, is that it has been associated with the heavy-handed humor and pathos of the plantation tradition and the minstrel show. For many phases of modern Negro

life this idiom is inappropriate, even if some of the principal characters might realistically be expected to speak in dialect. Johnson asserts
that the instrument of dialect has "but two full stops" (*BNP,* 41) and
is thus unable to render complexity. Later, when he added an addi-
tional preface to the second edition of the book (1931), he gladly
modified his stand, noting that some of the younger writers such as
Langston Hughes and Sterling A. Brown used dialect successfully in
their poetry. However, he distinguishes the dialect they use, "the
common, racy, living, authentic speech of the Negro in certain phases
of real life" (*BNP,* 4), from the hackneyed stage dialect of the late
nineteenth century.

Johnson closes his preface to the 1922 first edition of *The Book of
American Negro Poetry* by writing that he does not feel obliged to apol-
ogize for its contents, which represent not only the potential but the
genuine achievement of Negro poets. Part of the reason for his historical introduction has been to make clear "the distance already covered
. . . . from the plaints of George Horton to the invectives of Claude
McKay" (*BNP,* 47).

The preface to the 1931 edition added even more positive notes,
coming as it did at the end of the Harlem Renaissance that the first
edition had helped to launch. Looking back at the group of poets who
began to write at about the time of World War I, Johnson notes that
they had revolted against the constraints of dialect poetry, the stereotypes of Negro character and behavior, excessive sentiment, and the
pleading tone of nineteenth-century poets. Now there was an even
younger generation in revolt against these militant poets. The young
writers who had emerged during the renaissance were reacting to the
"protest, rebellion, and despair" (*BNP,* 5) of the World War I poets
and writing poetry that was free from propaganda. To some this
meant ignoring race altogether, a course that Johnson feels is unsuccessful because "an artist accomplishes his best when working at his
best with the material he knows best" (*BNP,* 7). But several emerging poets addressed the question of race without employing propaganda, and Johnson has only praise for such artists as Countee Cullen,
Langston Hughes, Sterling Brown, Helene Johnson, Arna Bontemps,
and Gwendolyn Bennett. One hopeful sign that he identifies is the
awareness of "genuine folk stuff" that Hughes displayed in his use of
blues and Sterling Brown in his use of the black tall tale and ballad
traditions that resulted in "folk epics" like "Stagolee" or "John
Henry" (*BNP,* 6). Thus in the second edition of his anthology John-

son sees great potential in the new generation of writers, who were expanding the traditions of black poetry. They maintained a healthy independence, not only toward the generation that came before them but toward their white audience. He looks to them to stand on their "racial foundation . . . to fashion something that rises above mere race and reaches out to the universal in truth and beauty" (*BNP,* 7).

The Negro Spirituals

One of the ambitions of Johnson's nameless protagonist in *The Autobiography of an Ex-Colored Man* was to record the music of black America. In the 1920s Johnson set out to do something similar, taking as his area of specialization the spirituals. Because of his experience in songwriting and his ready access to the material, no one was better suited for such a task. Not only did Johnson bring his own musical experience to the project, but he convinced his brother Rosamond and songwriter Lawrence Brown to do the musical arrangements for *The Book of American Negro Spirituals* (1925). Brought out by Viking Press in the middle of the Harlem Renaissance, the first collection of spirituals was sufficiently popular to encourage Viking and the Johnson brothers to bring out *The Second Book of Negro Spirituals* just one year later. Each book collected sixty-one songs, printing words and music.

The 1925 anthology contains a cross section of the best-known spirituals, including "Go Down Moses," "Joshua Fit de Battle ob Jerico," "Swing Low Sweet Chariot," "All God's Chillun Got Wings," "Deep River," "Steal Away to Jesus," and "Nobody Knows the Trouble I See." If the 1926 edition suffers by comparison, it nevertheless offers a number of very familiar songs, such as "In Dat Great Gittin' Up Mornin'," "Rise Up Shepherd An' Foller," "Sometimes I Feel Like a Motherless Child," and "Were You There When They Crucified My Lord?" interspersed with spirituals that were unfamiliar to white readers of the book.

As he had done with his anthology of poetry, Johnson prefaced the first collection with a lengthy critical essay designed to argue the importance of the contents as art and to explain the history and conventions of the spirituals. He begins by reproducing his own poem, "O Black and Unknown Bards," and by meditating upon it. The spirituals would have been remarkable, he suggests, even had they been written by the white settlers of the North American continent, who were faced with a hostile natural environment. However, these songs were created by a subculture of slaves, illiterate for the most part, who composed songs in a foreign language upon principles that had little to do with their original heritage. Johnson rejects the argument that the spirituals are largely derived from the religious music and folk songs of the white slaveholders. He points out that the Fisk Jubilee Singers had successfully toured Europe and that no European critics had discerned European origins for the music of the group.

Johnson proposes another theory for the origin of the spirituals, a theory that has been subject to controversy over the years.[3] Noting the importance of African painting and sculpture and their influence on the modern European and American arts, he argues that the spirituals owe a great deal to African traditions. African music is particularly noted for the complexity and sophistication of its rhythms, and Johnson feels that rhythm is the key to tracing the origins of the spirituals: "They have a striking rhythmic quality, and show a marked similarity to African songs in form and intervallic structure. But the spirituals . . . go a step in advance of African music through a higher melodic and an added harmonic development."[4] Aware that his readers might find the notion of African origin for these Christian songs hard to accept, Johnson cites scholarly research that had established ties between northern African music and Spanish music, particularly the Moorish habañera, which found its way into Spanish music and then into Bizet's *Carmen*. But the African rhythms are only the first component of the spirituals.

The other basic ingredient is Christianity. As Johnson points out, there were many reasons—especially the difference between theory and practice—why the newly arrived slaves might have chosen not to embrace the religion of their oppressors, but there were also sound reasons for their conversion. Chief among the latter was the appropriateness of the teachings of Christianity to the plight in which the slaves found themselves: "Far from his native land and customs, despised by those among whom he lived, experiencing the pang of the separation of loved ones, . . . feeling the lash, the Negro seized Christianity, the religion of compensations in the life to come for the ills suffered in the present existence. . ." (*BNS,* 20). One of the biblical books that seemed most appropriate to their own state was Exodus, and it is not surprising that American slaves should have identified with the people of Israel, hoping that the same God who led the Hebrews from bondage in Egypt would eventually deliver the Negro from his state.

Johnson moves next to the authorship of the songs, posing the insoluble question of whether they were the work of talented individuals or the product of spontaneous improvisation of the early congregations. Although no authoritative answer can be given, Johnson proposes that both factors were important. Just as in his own day he had seen itinerant singers lead congregations in song, supplying the "leading lines" while the congregation replied with the chorus, Johnson suggests that composers might have invented the basic songs, encouraged by the group, while the responses might well have been derived from the spontaneous outbursts of the congregations.

The very form of leading line and response is another characteristic of African music, and Johnson quotes from two African songs that follow the form, then juxtaposes "Oh Wasn't Dat a Wide Ribber" to illustrate the parallel. He speculates that the earliest of the spirituals probably followed this leading line-response form closely, while later songs developed "a true chorus," more complex than the simple response. "Steal Away to Jesus" is cited as an example of a third development. There is a chorus—

> Steal away, steal away,
> Steal away to Jesus.
> Steal away, steal away home,
> I ain't got long to stay here.
> (*BNS*, 26)

which is followed by the lines of the leader, and then finally by the simple response, "I ain't got long to stay here."

The rhythm of the spirituals, unlike that of black secular music, is based on the swinging of the head of the singer rather than on the clapping of hands or the tapping of feet as in secular music. This difference accounts for the fact that, while ragtime, blues, and jazz had been taken over by white musicians before or during the 1920s, the "feel" of the spirituals had so far eluded most white singers. Johnson states that even black singers were often unsuccessful when they attempted to "perform" the spirituals in a concert setting because the songs do not lend themselves to solo performance, and only such talented singers as Roland Hayes and Paul Robeson could successfully render them on the stage.

Johnson digresses briefly to write about black secular music and its ties to religious music. He recalls the "ring shouts" of his youth which combined the handclapping of secular music with a religious theme. Because the ministers and the more conservative members of the congregation considered the rhythms of the ring shouts too worldly, the shouts were usually indulged in after formal religious services were over, and eventually the black church banned the practice, so that by the time Johnson was compiling his anthology, the practice had nearly disappeared.

Discussing the singing of the spirituals, which differ from most folk music in that they are sung in harmony, Johnson again digresses to treat the prevalence of quartets among black youth at the turn of the century. As a boy he heard and sang in barbershop quartets. When he moved to New York and participated in musical comedy, the black quartet was a fixture of such shows, culminating in the popularity of *Shuffle Along* in 1921. Not all collectors of the spirituals had been aware that they were sung in harmony, Johnson notes, and some had gone so far as to deny the fact. The arrangers of Johnson's collection, however, had provided piano accompaniments that "give the characteristic harmonies that would be used in spontaneous group singing" (*BNS,* 37).

Johnson considers the lyrics of the spirituals less distinctive than the music. But despite the triteness and naiveté of some of the lines as well as the sometimes tiresome repetition, he feels that the lyrics contain much true poetry. Visual images abound, with color imagery added liberally to the biblical paraphrases that are the basis for the songs. The pathos of the folk composers softens the "austerity" of the original biblical language, producing a song that is more emotional than the language of the Bible; some songs are even leavened by humor.

Johnson viewed dialect as inappropriate in modern poetry; however, he preserved the dialect in which he found the spirituals. He warns that whites who expect a universal "Negro dialect" could be surprised, for dialects differ widely according to locale. Following the lead of Dunbar, he says that he has never distorted the spelling of words merely to render the songs exotic, but only to mark specific differences between black pronunciation and that of standard English. When dialect spellings would render a word completely unintelligible (he cites the pronunciation "sode" for "sword") he maintains the standard spelling of the word.

The introduction concludes with a survey of earlier anthologies of spirituals and with the observation that the 1920s were at last a period when these songs had come to enjoy a vogue because of the efforts of early collectors and the talent of recent interpreters of the songs. He might have added that the obsession of the 1920s artist and audience with "primitive" cultures and art forms was a major contributing factor. Johnson welcomes the renewed interest in spirituals as another sign of America's changing attitude toward the Negro and his contribution to American culture, a change that stemmed, he says, from the Negro's own increased self-respect.

Assuming that the reader is familiar with the earlier collection, the preface to *The Second Book of Negro Spirituals* is less informative than the first introduction. Johnson does note the peculiar absence of a great many "Christian Spirituals," songs treating the birth of Christ, although he includes some in this anthology. He surmises that this scarcity might be due to the fact that in the old South Christmas was less a religious holiday than a secular one, on which slaves were given a day off and liberally supplied with liquor and food. He briefly summarizes his earlier remarks about previous collectors of the songs and about the black contribution to secular music and dance. He closes, however, on a new note. Looking back at the "unknown bards" who composed the spirituals and forward to the generation of artists then emerging, Johnson speculates about the potential of the latter. While nothing as completely different as the spirituals might be produced, he feels that the songs pointed the way for the individual artist's real accomplishment, which would result from following the "racial genius" of the black American.

Johnson's collections of the spirituals did more than merely bring together 122 famous black religious songs. Coming as they did at the height of interest in black culture, the two volumes furthered the respect for the Negro that Johnson sought to engender by means of all his original and critical writings. Like *The Book of American Negro Poetry*, these two anthologies of spirituals both praise the race for the artistic progress that it has already made and encourage its artists to go on to further achievements.

Johnson's Critical Essays

Because of his prominence, Johnson found himself cast as a spokesman for the black artistic community during the 1920s and 1930s. The pressure of his work with the NAACP, his teaching, and his creative writing left him little time, but he did produce a handful of essays during these two decades. These writings may be divided into two categories: general articles, which praise black artistic contributions and attempt to bring them to the attention of the rest of the nation, and more specifically focused essays, which are addressed more to artists than to the general public and deal with the special problems and concerns of the black writer and artist. It is the latter class of essay in which Johnson makes the greater contribution to black letters. Sometimes, as in "Negro Authors and White Publishers," he treats a single specific point, while in an essay such as "The Dilemma of the Negro Author" he treats the gamut of problems faced by a black author.

"Negro Authors and White Publishers" appeared in the *Crisis* in 1929, almost at the end of the Harlem Renaissance, and addresses those black authors who claimed that their work was not published because "the leading white publishers have set a standard which Negro writers must conform to or go unpublished. . . ."[5] That standard, they complained, called for black characters to be depicted in condescending or degrading terms, for a concentration on the "lower types of Negroes," and for treatment only of the lower depths of black social life. Johnson disagrees with this contention, asserting that writing is seldom rejected because it is too good for the market. He examines some of the recent publishing successes scored by black authors: while six books deal with the lower socioeconomic scale—among them Claude McKay's *Home to Harlem* (1928) and *Banjo* (1929), Jean Toomer's *Cane* (1923), and Wallace Thurman's *The Blacker the Berry* (1929)—eight novels deal with black life on the "upper levels." Jessie Fauset, Walter White, and Nella Larsen had each published two novels set in middle-class black society; W. E. B. DuBois and Harry Liscomb had each published one. He compiles similar lists of prose nonfiction and poetry books, nineteen of which he classes as "upper level" literature against only two that depict the lower classes. His essay is a stern bit of advice for aspiring black authors, who should do their best work in the fields of their choice and stop complaining about the lack of publishing opportunity. Ironically Johnson's advice came just before the Depression, during which even some established authors such as Langston Hughes found it difficult to find publishers, but Johnson's essay was based on the positive experiences of the 1920s.

Although Johnson sounds complacent in the *Crisis* essay, two other articles show how fully he recognized the special problems of black writers. In "The Dilemma of the Negro Author" he states that they face the normal difficulties encountered by all writers, but also the "special problem . . . of the double audience; it is more than a double audience; it is a divided audience, an audience made up of two elements with differing and often opposite and antagonistic points of view."[6]

If the black author chooses to write chiefly for whites, he finds himself fighting the preconception that white America has about black Americans, the notion that they must belong to one of two stereotypes—what Sterling Brown would later come to call the "local color" Negro or the "brute Negro."[7] The black author finds it impossible either to work with the "stencils" of these two stereotypes or to make his white audience accept superior or noble black characters that completely contradict the stereotypes. Nor can he simply avoid the problem by writing instead about white society, for "white America does not welcome seeing the Negro competing with the white man on what it considers the white man's own ground."[8]

On the other hand, if the black author writes for the black audience, he is expected by the black press and clergy to depict only the most admirable traits of the race in his work. Black speakers may attack the race "for its faults and foibles and vices, " and even the black theater may burlesque those follies for wholly black audiences, but the writer, whose printed work may be read by the whites, is seen as betraying his race if he writes too frankly. Torn between his two audiences, the black writer becomes schizophrenic: "on one page black America is his whole or main audience, and on the very next page white America."[9]

The solution that Johnson offers is for the black writer to accept the fact of his divided audience and to attempt to set a middle course, primarily guided by his own integrity. Thus he will find himself breaking not only the stereotypes of the white reader but also the taboos of the black reader. If he is successful, he "will have something close to a common audience, and will be about as free from outside limitations as other writers."[10]

The positive note on which this essay ends is reinforced by "Race Prejudice and the Negro Artist," also published in 1928. There Johnson summarizes the literary achievements of black writers in the fields of poetry, drama, prose fiction, and nonfiction. These strides have been matched by the work of black actors and singers such as Charles Gilpin, Roland Hayes, and Paul Robeson. The creative achievements of a growing number of black artists, Johnson says, have dispelled the old American stereotype that the Negro "is here only to receive; to be shaped into something new and unquestionably better" by the civilizing force of white America.[11] The black artist "is making it realized that he is the possessor of a wealth of natural endowments and that he has long been a generous giver to America."[12] As the artist does his work, newspapers carry stories of black singers, actors, and writers rather than negative accounts of black criminals. The black artist, then, has a significance that is larger than the artistic success of his creation. He has in his hands the ability to change forever the way in which his race is regarded by the nation.

Johnson's contribution to the literary life of black America would have been great had he written no poetry or fiction of his own. By collecting and introducing *The Book of American Negro Poetry, The Book of American Negro Spirituals,* and *The Second Book of Negro Spirituals,* he brought a great body of creative work by black artists to the attention of the divided audience of which he wrote. He encouraged black Americans to respect their culture and achievements, and he made it necessary for white Americans to respect the Negro.

Chapter Five
Historian and Political Activist

Toward the end of the 1920s the strain of Johnson's work with the NAACP began to catch up with him. As early as 1925 his doctor had warned him to slow down, but in 1927, when his assistant Walter White took a year's leave to accept a Guggenheim fellowship, Johnson had to increase his pace just to keep up with his work. Following an extended illness in the spring of 1929, he was able to take time off from the organization and accept a grant from the Rosenwald Fund.[1] The chief work completed during his tenure as a Rosenwald fellow during 1929-1930 was a book that he had been planning for some time, a history of black people in New York City. By 1934, however, Johnson entered the civil rights field once again with the publication of *Negro Americans, What Now?*

Black Manhattan

The notion of writing a history of black New York was not new to Johnson in 1929. In 1925 he had written an essay, "The Making of Harlem," for a special Harlem number of *Survey Graphic*. There he traced the history of black settlement in New York back to the city's Dutch period, recounted the efforts of early black Harlemites to rent or buy property, and stressed the unique nature of Harlem among black settlements in the United States. Because of the nature of employment in New York, the most recent black immigrant from other areas found himself thrown into the city's polyglot culture and assimilated much more quickly than black migrants who worked in all-black crews, as they did in the Chicago stockyards or the Pittsburgh steel mills, for example. This assimilation was even more complete than in the case of recent white immigrants such as German Jews or Italians, where the language of the immigrant's quarter separated him from New York culture. Johnson's pride in the black population of Harlem is evident when he cites the area as a "laboratory" that disproves the myth that "if Negroes were transported to the North in large numbers the race problem with all its acuteness and with new aspects would be transferred with them."[2] He notes that the crime rate in Harlem was no worse than in the rest of the city and that, after initial white resistance to the black "invasion," whites had dealt with the Negroes of Harlem fairly and peaceably. He closes the essay with the prediction that Harlem is destined to become "the intellectual, the cultural and the financial center for Negroes of the United States."[3] Alain Locke, who had edited the special number of *Survey Graphic* in which Johnson's essay appeared, soon included it in his influential anthology *The New Negro* (1925), where it was entitled "Harlem: The Culture Capital."

When he set out to write a book-length history of Harlem, Johnson found that some of his themes extended beyond New York, as when he wrote of political movements and artistic developments, but he unified the book by making sure that "the main threads of interest led out from New York or from without back to it."[4] The result was a book that was not only a far better history of black New York than Johnson modestly claimed, but a study of black achievements throughout much of the United States from colonial days to the late 1920s.

Black Manhattan opens with the year 1626, when New Amsterdam was founded by the Dutch governor, Peter Minuit, and the total Negro population of the area consisted of eleven men, only four of whom are known by name. He follows the growth of the black population through the abolition of slavery in New York State in 1827—the next census in 1830 recorded a black population of 14,083 Negroes living in New York City—and closes with the post-World-War-I period when a single protest parade mustered ten thousand Harlemites. The history of Harlem begins and ends with violence directed against black people. In 1705 the General Assembly of the State of New York passed a law restricting the travel of slaves to prevent their escaping to Canada, and by 1712 relations between the races were bad enough to cause a "Negro Insurrection" which resulted in the violent deaths of nine whites and the execution of twenty-one Negroes. Near the end of his history Johnson describes the silent parade protesting lynching in 1917. Yet despite the grim nature of some of the facts he presents, he remains optimistic about the eventual triumph of right. He maintains throughout the book that the New York Negro has advanced greatly during the three hundred years of his history on Manhattan Island and will continue to advance.

One reason for the progress of the black race is found in Johnson's record of a combination of social agitation and self-help, led by a handful of active individuals and organizations. He illustrates the early resistance to slavery by members of the free black community with the story of James Hamlet, the first slave to face extradition under the Fugitive Slave Act. When Hamlet was arrested in New York City just eight days after passage of the bill, black people of New York gathered at Zion Church, not only to denounce the law, but to raise eight hundred dollars to buy Hamlet's freedom. Black New Yorkers were active in their support of the Underground Railroad to aid escaping slaves; more important, they looked to the future by building strong social organizations that would advance the cause of the race after the Civil War.

A free school system was one such organization. Aided by sympathetic Quakers, who had voluntarily renounced slavery long before its abolition, black New Yorkers opened an African Free School in 1787; interestingly, this school was founded a number of years before any free school existed for white children Although the first teachers were white, a cadre of black teachers had formed by 1834, when there were seven African Free Schools in the city. Johnson stresses the value of the free schools during the nineteenth century: "It was due mainly to them that there was produced in New York City and State a body of intelligent and well-trained coloured men and women ready to assume leadership during the great crisis in the history of their race" (*BM,* 23). But the schools were not the sole influential institution that led New York blacks from bondage to freedom.

The black church also aided the black cause. Apart from the spiritual solace they offered, the black congregations of the city were social institutions that constituted a ready-made platform from which some of the great black orators of the century and any number of lesser leaders addressed large audiences. Johnson points out that the phenomenal growth of the black church was once again the ironic fruit of segregation and discrimination against blacks. Black members of white congregations were forced to sit in Jim Crow galleries and had to take communion separately, after all the whites. Such abuses led to the early establishment of black churches, which soon became more significant and powerful within the black community than any white church could have been. The ransoming of James Hamlet, mentioned earlier, is a primary example of the sort of immediate social action that could be accomplished by the church.

By the beginning of the twentieth century, purely secular organiza-

tions for the betterment of black people emerged, among them the
Citizen's Protective League, founded in 1900, the Niagara Movement
(1905), and the National Association for the Advancement of Colored
People (1910), the organization to which Johnson gave so much of
his life. Although the leadership of the NAACP was largely white for
its first few years, it might never have been founded had it not been
for the earlier organizing efforts of black leaders such as W. E. B.
DuBois and T. Thomas Fortune, publisher of the *New York Age*.

Fortune, DuBois, and other leaders were following a tradition that
is another part of black New York's history, as Johnson makes clear.
Frederick Douglass lived in the city during much of his career, and
Johnson claims him as a New Yorker. Sojourner Truth, originally
from Ulster County, was living in New York City when she had the
vision that led to her career as an orator. For Harriet Tubman the city
was a base from which to launch her nineteen missions as a guide for
the Underground Railroad in the South. Whether they were major
personalities such as these or merely anonymous financial contributors
such as the fifteen hundred who made up James Hamlet's ransom,
New York Negroes had a long history of helping the less fortunate
members of their race to fight slavery and to win their rights as citizens in the stormy period following the Civil War.

Johnson emphasizes that the New York Negroes' contributions to
American history were not limited to the political scene. During the
Civil War New York State furnished four of the 161 regiments of
black troops raised by the Union, providing valuable propaganda for
black people since "sentiment for the Negro and his cause was
strengthened by the fact that black men were fighting and dying both
to save the Union and to free the slaves" (*BM*, 50). The eagerness of
black men to enlist and their subsequent valor in combat were particularly notable during a period in which military conscription was vio-
lently resisted by some white New Yorkers; the Draft Riots of 1863,
for example, saw the destruction of the city's draft headquarters and
the hanging of a number of Negroes who were caught by the mob.
The end result was "a flood of kindly feeling towards the Negro and
of indignation against the mob. Within a few months a regiment of
Negro troops, raised and equipped by the Union League Club,
marched down Broadway on their way to the front escorted by leading
citizens and cheered by thousands that lined the sidewalks" (*BM*, 53).
Again in World War I the results of black patriotism were bitter-
sweet. Enlistments in a proposed black regiment of the New York
National Guard were met with the state assembly's reluctance to cre-

ate the regiment, and when it did form, the Fifteenth Regiment was sent for training to South Carolina, where racial friction resulted in hard feelings between the troops and local citizens. Once in France, however, the Fifteenth was cited for "exceptional valour in action" by the French government, and the regiment received a heroes' welcome from white New York as well as Harlem.

While Johnson covers such historical topics as the fight against slavery and the participation of black New Yorkers in the political and military life of the city, his major interests are obviously in other areas, as evidenced by the fact that he devotes ten of his twenty chapters to social and cultural topics, principally black involvement in journalism, sports, the theater, and literature.

Journalism was one of the first fields in which black New Yorkers distinguished themselves. Led by John B. Russworm, who founded *Freedom's Journal* in 1827, black journalists eventually established eight abolitionist newspapers in New York City before the Civil War. While the abolition of slavery brought an end to this first flowering of the black press in New York, the twentieth century saw the establishment of a host of magazines published by black organizations. Johnson mentions not only those journals that contributed to the artistic and cultural life of black New York—journals including the *Crisis, Opportunity,* and *Survey Graphic*—but a group of radical publications. Although the *Messenger, Challenge,* the *Voice,* the *Crusader,* the *Emancipator,* and the *Negro World* were considered evidence of sedition among Negroes by the Justice Department in 1919, and although Johnson was not personally sympathetic toward their views, he contends that they did some good since they "shook up the Negroes of New York and the country and effected some changes that have not been lost. . . ." (*BM,* 251). He also reveals a grudging admiration for the "forcible and trenchant English, the precise style" (*BM,* 246) of the radical journalists.

Less controversial contributions to popular culture were provided by black New York athletes. Johnson devotes an early chapter to the activities of jockeys, baseball players, and boxers active from the early years of the nineteenth century through the beginning of the twentieth. If the subject matter of this chapter seems less momentous than that of the political chapters, Johnson feels that it is nevertheless important, that black athletes made their contribution: "In New York the Negro now began to function and express himself on a different plane, in a different sphere; and in a different way he effectively impressed himself upon the city and the country" (*BM,* 59). Black ath-

letes countered beliefs about black inferiority by excelling in their
sports, a fact that was not lost on the white promoters and players of
those sports. In baseball the teams were segregated to minimize the
chance that comparisons between black athletes and their white team-
mates would demean the whites. Black teams did play white teams
rather often in early New York and acquitted themselves well. Financial gain was a factor that worked both for and against the black athlete: Johnson notes that the phenomenal success of black jockeys came
to an end when horse racing became popular enough to offer large
purses to winning jockeys, at which point white jockeys crowded out
black.

But it was in boxing that the black athlete made the greatest name
for himself. The fighter was dependent only on his personal ability
and not, like baseball players and jockeys, on fellow team members
or the mounts they rode. Johnson traces the history of black prize-
fighting back to Thomas Molineaux, a former slave from Virginia
who moved to New York after gaining his freedom in the early years
of the nineteenth century. By 1809, having beaten every fighter in
America, white or black, Molineaux was considered the American
champion, though there was no official title at the time, just as there
were no weight classes. Molineaux twice fought Tom Cribb, the British champion, for the world championship title, but was defeated
both times.

In addition to a number of other black fighters, Johnson treats the
career of the most spectacular black fighter up to his day, Jack Johnson. Although Johnson had lost the championship to Jess Willard
fifteen years before the publication of *Black Manhattan,* he was still a
major racial hero in 1930 because he had so forcefully debunked the
myth of white superiority: "A good part of the press and some literary
fellows were industrious in fomenting the sentiment that the security
of white civilization and white supremacy depended upon the defeat
of Jack Johnson. One of these writers assumed the role of both
prophet and comforter and before the Reno battle [with Jim Jeffries]
wrote in the red-blooded style of the day that Jeffries was bound to
win because, while he had Runnymede and Agincourt behind him,
the Negro had nothing but the jungle; that the Negro would be
licked the moment the white man looked him in the eye" (*BM,* 66).
Jack Johnson, of course, won an easy victory over Jeffries and became
a role model for multitudes of black boys and men.

More chapters are devoted to the various aspects of black show
business than to any other topic, hardly a surprising fact in view of

Johnson's involvement with musical comedy. The first cluster of chapters, 8 through 11, deals with black performers during the nineteenth century and with the history of black musical comedy, while a second cluster, 15 through 17, treats both the Negro in drama and the role of the black playwright in the twentieth century, primarily during the 1920s.

Black theatrical tradition, Johnson points out, began most respectably in New York with the performances of the African Company during the 1820s. The African Company performed both Shakespeare and brief "comic acts" for mixed audiences. This tradition of reviving the classics produced Ira Aldridge, who progressed to the stages of Dublin, London, and St. Petersburg. Another influence on the black theater was the minstrel tradition, which emerged from the South. By the 1860s black minstrels had progressed from impromptu performances on plantations to the stage with the formation of Lew Johnson's Plantation Minstrel Company. Although he recognizes the importance of the minstrel tradition to the emergence of black theater, Johnson also has reservations about it. "Minstrelsy was, on the whole, a caricature of Negro life, and it fixed a stage tradition which has not yet been entirely broken. It fixed the tradition of the Negro as only an irresponsible, happy-go-lucky, wide-grinning, loud-laughing, shuffling, banjo-playing, singing, dancing sort of being. Nevertheless, these companies did provide stage training and theatrical experience for a large number of coloured men . . . which, at the time, could not have been acquired from any other source" (*BM*, 93). Although Johnson does not draw the parallel explicitly, his criticism of the minstrel shows is almost identical to his reservation about dialect poetry: while both opened doors for black artists and resulted in noteworthy accomplishments, neither produced art of a very high order.

Johnson identifies the second period in the evolution of black theater, deriving from the minstrel shows, as characterized by elaborate musical shows featuring black women performers, beginning in 1890 with Sam T. Jack's *The Creole Show* and leading eventually to the musical comedies of Johnson, his brother Rosamond, and Bob Cole. In the evolution of the black stage show from the 1890s to the early years of the twentieth century, plots were increasingly emphasized until the shows became fully developed musical comedies. An important early show of this type, and a direct forerunner of the Cole and Johnson shows, was *Clorindy—The Origin of the Cake-Walk* (1898) by Will Marion Cook and Paul Laurence Dunbar. Although shows such

as Cook's *Jes Lak White Folks* or Cole and Johnson's *A Trip to Coontown*
may not sound far removed from the minstrel tradition, they depended on the genuine comedy of black writers and performers rather
than on a false tradition foisted upon them by blackface performers.
The period from 1900 to 1920 saw the popularization of the cakewalk, black folk music, jazz, and blues, not only among the whites
of America but in England and on the Continent. Nor was serious
music completely neglected during the period. Sissieretta Jones made
a name for herself on the concert stage, eventually performing at the
White House before President Benjamin Harrison. The classic and
popular traditions were united when she starred in *Black Patti's Trou-
badors,* a show written especially for her by Bob Cole. This period of
development eventually culminated in the theatrical manifestation of
the Harlem Renaissance during the 1920s.

   Johnson identifies a third period of theatrical development, from
about 1910 to 1917: Negro shows lost favor on Broadway and a new
black theatrical tradition took root in Harlem, with shows produced
by and for black people, rather than for predominantly white audiences as had been the case previously. This change in audience meant
freedom from certain taboos—for example, the requirement that romantic love scenes between black characters be treated only through
broad comedy. By the beginning of the Harlem Renaissance black
musical comedy, Shakespearean drama, and serious contemporary
drama all flourished in the theaters of Harlem. Johnson feels that the
excellence of some black acting encouraged white dramatists such as
Eugene O'Neill, Paul Green, and Marc Connelly to write plays featuring black characters. Although Johnson hailed the production of
Garland Anderson's *Appearances* as a major step toward putting the
black playwright on an equal footing with white authors, he had to
admit that, by the end of the 1920s, "The Negro as a writer for the
theatre has not kept pace; he has, in fact, lost ground. . . . Coloured
people often complain about the sort of light that is shed upon the
race in most Negro plays. It may be . . . that their remedy lies in
the development of Negro playwrights" (*BM,* 225).

   Meanwhile, though, great strides had been made during the 1920s
by black actors, singers, and musicians. The period produced such
major talents in serious drama as Paul Robeson and Charles Gilpin;
such renowned singers as Florence Mills, Josephine Baker, and Bessie
Smith; and such notable composers as Eubie Blake and Noble Sissle.
On the whole, before 1920 actors on stage were more successful than
writers for the stage.

During the 1920s, however, success came to many writers of non-dramatic literature, as Johnson acknowledges in chapter 19. After outlining the difficulties faced by pre-twentieth-century black poets and their failure to find a major audience, he reviews the prominent figures of the past decade. He identifies Claude McKay as the precursor of the recent movement and modestly notes his own contribution of editing *The Book of American Negro Poetry*. But he updates the introduction to the volume by treating the new generation of poets who had emerged between the publication of that anthology in 1922 and the end of the decade. Countee Cullen had distinguished himself by writing not only raceless lyric poems but a body of work that treated racial tensions in thought-provoking and beautiful verse. Langston Hughes's more earthy poetry had elevated the themes and techniques of the blues into high art. New prose writers as diverse as Jean Toomer, Walter White, Jessie Fauset, Nella Larsen, Rudolph Fisher, and Wallace Thurman had published from one to three books each during the years since 1920. Both the *Crisis* and *Opportunity* had made an effort to help the latest generation of creative writers by sponsoring contests and prizes that would attract new talents such as Zora Neale Hurston and Arna Bontemps, both of whom moved to Harlem because it seemed the logical place for an aspiring black writer to live during the 1920s.

Reflecting with pleasure on the success enjoyed by literary artists at the end of the Harlem Renaissance, Johnson looks forward to the day when the visual arts will catch up. Writing at the end of the 1920s, he did not know that the renaissance was coming to an end or that the Depression would cause economic and social losses for black people. Instead, he closes with the optimistic observation that, while "the Negro in New York still has far, very far yet, to go and many, very many, things yet to gain . . . New York guarantees her Negro citizens the fundamental rights of citizenship and protects them in the exercise of those rights. Possessing the basic rights, the Negro in New York ought to be able to work through the discriminations and disadvantages" (*BM*, 284).

Most contemporary reviewers of *Black Manhattan* noted what Johnson himself admits in the preface: that he was not really a historian, and that the strictly historical matter of the book could have been produced by any competent researcher. The strength of the book lay in the passages where Johnson relied on his own personal experience and his areas of expertise—the seven chapters on black theater, music, and literature, and chapter 18, where his NAACP experience was directly relevant. These eight chapters are strong enough to earn *Black Manhattan* a lasting place as a chronicle of the Harlem Renaissance and its antecedents.

Negro Americans, What Now?

In December 1930 Johnson, who had been on leave from his NAACP post to write *Black Manhattan,* resigned to accept the Adam K. Spence Chair of Creative Literature and Writing at Fisk University in Nashville, Tennessee. Because he had obtained an extension of his Rosenwald grant, he did not begin his teaching immediately, but worked on his revision of *The Book of American Negro Poetry* and the beginnings of his autobiography. In January 1932, two years after the announcement of his appointment, Johnson finally began his tenure at Fisk, where he was to teach during the winter and spring quarters each year, offering courses on American literature, the Negro in American literature, and creative writing.[5] It was a peaceful time, with leisure for the writing that Johnson could not do when he was embroiled in the controversies of the NAACP. But he was not yet finished with the activist period of his life. From his retreat in Nashville he attempted to distill what he had learned in his years with the NAACP and apply it to the current problems of his race. The result was a 100-page essay published by Viking in 1934.

Negro Americans, What Now? acknowledges that the world of 1934 was a far different one from that of the 1920s, when it appeared that the fortunes of the black race were on the rise. Johnson sees the world in a state of "semi-chaos" brought about by the Depression, and he recognizes that black Americans have become confused as to which way they should turn for a solution to their problems. In the three sections of the book he reviews the options that have always been open to black people ("Choices"), takes stock of their strengths ("Forces and Resources"), and maps out the beginnings of a strategy for the 1930s ("Techniques and Policies").

In "Choices" Johnson first treats two approaches to the racial question that have failed in the past—exodus and physical force—and then examines current options. He samples emigration schemes from the establishment of Liberia in the early nineteenth century to the Garvey movement of the 1920s, and rejects exodus as a possible option. Nor does physical force appeal to him except as a last resort in response to mob action. As Johnson has learned from history, the slave insurrections merely resulted in worse treatment for all black people, not in any liberalization of slavery. One modern solution being offered is communism; Johnson professes to have no prejudices against communism but finds it unsuitable as a solution to the racial problems of the United States. He correctly foresees that communism will not become a dominant force in the United States and suggests that by joining the movement the Negro will make himself more of an outcast than ever.

This line of reasoning brings Johnson to what he feels are the only options left—isolation or integration. By isolation he means "the making of the race into a self-contained economic, social, and cultural unit."[6] Although throughout Johnson's life the majority of black people had been integrationists, he admits that the frustrations inherent in working toward integration and being constantly rebuffed can lead even the most rational thinker to give up and embrace isolationism. He cites his longtime colleague W. E. B. DuBois as an example of such discouragement. But he feels that there is no possibility "of our being able to duplicate the economic and social machinery of the country" (*NA,* 15). Thus, integration is the only viable alternative left for black Americans.

The bulk of his book is devoted to assessing the strengths of the race and determining how these resources should be used. As he points out, twelve million people should be able to achieve major goals if they can remain united. Too often, however, they have allowed themselves to be split into factions. As Johnson sees it, the race must use the black church, black press, and black fraternal organizations to inform their constituencies and to unite them in political action. These various organizations can complement what Johnson calls a "super-power," a racial organization that will focus the energies of the race and its smaller organized units on specific goals for the entire race. Not surprisingly, he concludes that the NAACP is the logical organization to fill the "super-power" role.

In "Techniques and Policies" Johnson looks at the activities that should occupy the race. First on his agenda is education, not only the formal education of black youth but the informal education of prejudiced whites. He is suspicious of vocational education because the skills learned can so easily become obsolete. Generally for black students he favors a sound academic education supplemented by special courses such as black history. But Johnson puts little faith in the willingness of the educational establishment to eliminate prejudice in white students. What he somewhat naively suggests as a grass-roots technique is that each American Negro adopt some white "pupil" and send him articles and books that will attack his prejudices by advancing sensible arguments or citing positive examples of black people. In Johnson's view political activity is another path to advancement. While many black Americans were still unable to register and vote in 1934, progress was being made in some areas of the country, and Johnson advises black people to vote wherever they are legally able to do so and to be more concerned with races for local offices than with national contests. He wisely points out that, practically speaking, it may be more important to a black man in the South to have a fair-minded county sheriff than to have the president of his choice. He cautions against allowing the Republican party to count on receiving the national black vote; if black voters are independent, both parties will have to take steps to win their votes. Johnson's experiences in attempting to pass antilynching legislation through Congress in the 1920s had estranged him from the party he had worked for as a young man.

In "Labor and Business" Johnson addresses one of the major concerns of the thirties—the lack of jobs. Jobs that had traditionally been held by blacks in the South had disappeared. During hard times even collecting garbage was considered a suitable job for a white man, so that black unemployment had risen even faster than the general rate of unemployment. Labor unions had only made the situation worse for black workers by excluding them. Johnson advocates negotiation with the union leadership, backed up by the possibility of boycotts or "scabbing," to convince the unions to accept black members. He also calls on the NAACP to enforce the rights of the largest group of black workers in America, the sharecroppers of the South. Finally, the creation of more black businesses would generate more jobs. In keeping with the policy he had earlier enunciated against isolationism, he stresses that black businessmen should not expect automatic loyalty from black customers, nor should they fail to offer their services to white customers.

Near the end of the book Johnson cautions against distrust of well-meaning white people and black leaders. He suggests, "If a white person takes that one step forward, let us not rail at him for not taking two or a dozen steps or not coming all the way; but let us give him due credit for the one step taken" (*NA*, 84). Among black people, black leaders are subject to almost as much scorn as well-meaning whites, for "lambasting our leaders is quite a popular pastime" (*NA*, 85–86). Johnson knew whereof he spoke, having been a leader during the antilynching campaigns of the 1920s. He was also keenly aware of criticism leveled at the NAACP as he was writing *Negro Americans, What Now?* He reminds his readers that if leadership imposes great responsibilities on the leader, the followers have their responsibilities as well. They should not be led away from their true leaders by "every loud-mouthed demagogue or smooth-tongued charlatan who comes along" (*NA*, 90), a probable allusion to figures as diverse as Marcus Garvey, head of the Universal Negro Improvement Association, and the proponents of the Communist Party of the United States.

A personal cause surfaces near the end of the book when Johnson considers the creation of stereotypes in literature. To correct the picture of the Negro as a "lazy, shiftless, unreliable . . . child, a pathetically good-humored buffoon" or "a brutal and degenerate criminal" (*NA*, 91), the black writer must contradict these stereotypes. But the black writer is often economically unsuccessful because black people do not buy and read books in sufficient numbers. Johnson urges the support of the literary arts by black readers, who might thus lend moral as well as financial support to writers.

Johnson closes *Negro Americans* with inspirational words. The chief consolation of black people in the United States should be the knowledge that they are in the right, fighting for a just cause. This knowledge should enable them to persevere even in times as hostile to their cause as the 1920s. Finally, he urges his readers to take as their motto his own credo: that is, never allow the prejudice of another person to blight one's own life.

Judgments

Johnson's two books of nonfiction evoked very different responses from the reviewers. *Black Manhattan* was well received by both the black press and mainstream publications. The prestigious *Journal of Negro History,* though acknowledging the popular tone of *Black Manhattan,* praised the work for its record of stage history. The *New York Times Book Review* and the *New York Herald Tribune* responded very favorably. Writing for the *New York Evening Post,* W. E. B. DuBois called the book the "best contribution ever made to the history of American Negro art, and especially the drama."[7]

Negro Americans, What Now? was also treated well by the white press. Reviewers for publications such as the *Saturday Review* praised it as speaking reasonably to both races. However, a review by W. E. B. DuBois suggests that the conciliatory and calm tone of the book might have been more appealing to white than to black readers of the 1930s. DuBois, who had recently moved toward the communist camp, saw the book as a reflection of Johnson's old-fashioned notion of leadership and argued that his former colleague did not really understand economics and failed to realize the necessity of breaking down the capitalistic system.[8]

As a writer of nonfiction, Johnson is sure and accomplished, but these polemical works do not represent him at his best. While both make a certain contribution to black history, neither adds a great deal to his reputation as a creative writer. The nonfiction work written between these two, on the other hand, is one of Johnson's best books. *Along This Way,* the major fruit of the period between his resignation from the NAACP and his assumption of the chair at Fisk, allowed him the freedom to carry some of his literary techniques into the field of autobiography.

Chapter Six
Along This Way

Johnson remarks in *Along This Way* that one reason for writing his autobiography was the tendency for readers of his novel, *The Autobiography of an Ex-Colored Man,* to confuse him with his fictional protagonist. However, autobiography is an important genre in Afro-American literature, and Johnson would probably have written an autobiography even without such a specific stimulus. A staple of the abolitionist movement was the slave narrative, frequently written not by the slave himself but by a white abolitionist. *Along This Way* was also preceded by many impressive genuine autobiographies, such as the *Narrative* of Olaudiah Equiano (Gustavus Vassa), published in 1789; the three autobiographical books published by Frederick Douglass from 1845 to 1881; William Wells Brown's extensive autobiographical introduction to *Clotel* (1853); and Booker T. Washington's *Up From Slavery* (1901). Since the publication of Johnson's book, the genre has grown even more popular, and includes such best-sellers as Richard Wright's *Black Boy* (1945), *The Autobiography of Malcolm X* (1965), and Eldridge Cleaver's *Soul on Ice* (1968). One characteristic of the genre is that autobiography allows the writer to record and reflect upon his own life story, often drawing from it lessons for the instruction of the reader. In addition, black autobiography specifically awakens pride in the black reader by displaying the positive example of a member of his own race who has achieved some sort of distinction.

False Starts

Before Johnson could write the reasonable public book that *Along This Way* was to be, he first had to purge his system of the accumulated bitterness and cynicism stored up during his years as an NAACP executive. Among his working papers on the book are a number of surprising notes on his opinions of the South and on the psychology of white people. His gentlemanly demeanor and coolness in emotional situations belied the anger that must sometimes have smoldered under his placid exterior, but the anger is evident in his notes, particularly in his remarks about the impossibility of reforming the South or about the sexual peculiarities of white people, especially white women.

The facts that Johnson had grown up in the South, had been educated there, and had campaigned successfully in that region for the NAACP did not keep him from writing, at the end of his public career, "Many southerners I know and like—but so far as I am concerned the whole damned South, as an institution, can drop through the bottom of Hell."[1] At times he saw his attitude as a major limiting factor that might keep him from writing an effective autobiography at all: "Southern white people—as a whole—I hate so cordially it is going to be very difficult for me to be fair with them."[2] Stemming from this attitude was the determination to make it clear to whites that the salvation of his race lay not in imitations of the white man, "even in the white man's best qualities,"[3] but in the achievements of black people independent of the white race.

Johnson frequently comments on the sexual basis of racial prejudice, anticipating the later observations of writers from Calvin Hernton *(Sex and Racism in America)* to Eldridge Cleaver *(Soul on Ice)*. As Johnson saw the complex question, white men were jealous of the supposed sexual superiority of black men and did all they could to repress that sexuality. White women really felt that black men were more attractive than white men but attempted to deny their attraction by professing their fear and loathing of Negro men. Johnson's usual restraint is absent in his treatment of sexual matters in his notes, but when he wrote his final draft of *Along This Way,* he allowed dramatic events to speak for themselves instead of patently stating his own philosophy.

What finally emerged from his notes was a statement of the true direction of the autobiography: "The Negro has beaten the white man at a *vital* point in the game of life—the achieving of happiness—in spite of the white man's vaunted civilization."[4] Even this thesis, however, would be advanced with the restraint that marks most of Johnson's public writings.

Johnson tells the story of his life from his birth to the early 1930s, emphasizing the thrift, ambition, and devotion to education that characterized his immediate forebears as well as himself. His story is not just the story of his own life, but "an outline, a sketch, an impression . . . of what America has looked like to me through the years of my life."[5] The autobiographical Johnson engages in a lifelong fight against racial discrimination and violence, a fight characterized not by physical counterattacks but by firm and deliberate pressure within the legal system of the United States. In this dimension, the public Johnson is a representative man, pointing the way to others of his race. Since Johnson, in spite of the many other careers that he pursued, always thought of himself first as a writer, *Along This Way* is also the autobiography of an artist, relating the circumstances under which his various literary works were composed and often giving useful insights into the purposes behind them. Finally, *Along This Way* presents a personal picture of Johnson the man. The desire to write a frank autobiography was at war with his notion of decorum—and the latter won out, causing him to excise some of those thoughts that might have alienated readers of the 1930s; nevertheless, the book as published achieves Johnson's main goals. It is leavened with an engaging sense of humor that partially conceals irony, and, like most self-portraits, *Along This Way* is occasionally retouched deftly to show its writer in a somewhat better light.

Positive Examples

Unlike Frederick Douglass and Booker T. Washington, who begin their autobiographies with stories of severe hardships endured during their early years, Johnson begins with a description of his stable middle-class home. In the opening pages of *Along This Way* he suggests the reasons for the success of his forebears. On his mother's side, Stephen Dillet, Johnson's grandfather, had landed in Nassau with no possessions but the clothing he wore and a silver spoon that had been given to him, but he worked his way from an apprenticeship in a tailor's shop to important political posts in the Bahamas, serving as chief inspector of the police department, postmaster of Nassau, deputy adjutant general of the militia, and member of the House of Assembly, the legislature of the islands. Johnson knew less about his father's side of the family, but he admired his father for his ambition. James Johnson had started out as a waiter in New York City but became headwaiter at the Royal Victoria Hotel in Nassau and later at the St. James Hotel in Jacksonville, Florida. The elder Johnson invested his money wisely in Jacksonville real estate and developed a solid reputation in that city for financial stability and probity. Johnson's maternal grandmother, who had enjoyed comfortable ease in the Bahamas, cheerfully supported herself as a laundress and as proprietor of her own bakery in Jacksonville, and Johnson took pride in her considerable skill in both businesses. Ambition, hard work, and the wise use of assets were stressed by both sides of his family as Johnson was growing up.

But success in the Johnson family was not considered complete as long as it was only material success. Johnson's father devoted much time in his later years to serving as a lay minister. The Johnsons were of the intellectual and economic class identified by W. E. B. DuBois as the "talented tenth," and they were keenly aware of their obligations to black people less fortunate than themselves. Atlanta University, with its emphasis on service, strengthened this spirit in James Weldon Johnson.

Perhaps the greatest obligation imposed on Johnson was that of setting a proper example for those who would observe him. Role models for aspiring black children were scarce in the latter years of the nineteenth century, and Johnson makes it clear that he thought of himself as a potential model by emphasizing others who were the first to accomplish something and by reminding his readers of his own considerable list of firsts. His grandfather, Stephen Dillet, was the first black man elected to the House in the Bahamas; the House at first refused to seat him, but Dillet persisted, was seated, and was returned to office for thirty years. Johnson's mother was the first black woman to teach in the public schools of Florida. Johnson himself, soon after his graduation from Atlanta University, became the first black person to pass a bar examination in the state of Florida and founded the first black daily newspaper. In later life he was one of the first songwriters to break into the New York musical world and became the first black secretary of the NAACP. Rather than selfish egotism, Johnson's pride in his own accomplishments and in those of his family was rooted in his belief that they represented achievements not so much of individuals as of his race.

Johnson articulates his feeling of being a representative of an entire race early in *Along This Way* when he tells of assuming the principalship of Stanton School immediately after his graduation from Atlanta University. He reports that he was keenly aware of the importance of his making good. A white principal doing a mediocre job in a white school could easily be overlooked, but a black man doing a bad job would be taken as evidence that all black people were inferior, that they were incapable of administrative duties.

Johnson also counters assumptions of black inferiority throughout his autobiography by reporting positive aspects of black life and positive attitudes toward his race that he encountered in others or discovered in his own consciousness. Thus, like Thoreau's *Walden, Along*

This Way is not only a record of what happened to its author, but a spiritual autobiography and a record of his observations and thoughts as he traveled "along his way."

One story that Johnson tells about his youth serves as a sort of metaphor for the humble place black people have traditionally occupied in American society and the unexpected resources they have to offer that society. When Johnson was kept out of the university by the yellow fever epidemic of 1888 and his father suggested a tutor, Johnson was taken aback by the unprepossessing appearance of the man and his surroundings:

We went to see this man and found him in a small, dingy, cobbler's shop that he ran, pegging away at old shoes. He was a little man, very black, partially bald, with a scraggly beard, and but for bright, intelligent eyes an insignificant presence. At the sight of the surroundings my heart misgave me, and I was embarrassed both for my father and myself. I wondered if he misunderstood so much as to think that I wanted to be coached in spelling and arithmetic and geography. I was reassured when the little cobbler began to talk. He spoke English as no professor at the University could speak it. (A, 92–93)

With this unpretentious teacher Johnson studied geometry and Latin, and he later had occasion to compare this tutor's educational approach to the classics with the approaches of his professors at Atlanta. The cobbler, he reported, made each class a lesson in the history and politics of the time as well as an exercise in translation, while his university teachers made the Greek plays Johnson studied mere "exercises in Greek grammar" (A, 93). In fact, the only teacher Johnson found to be the equal of this unassuming cobbler was Professor Brander Matthews, with whom he studied at Columbia University.

While most of the lessons embedded in the text of *Along This Way* are not so dramatic as the anecdote of the cobbler, Johnson never misses a chance to reverse stereotypical notions of the nature of black Americans. When he remembers his childhood in Jacksonville, he recalls seeing black members of the Florida militia, veterans of an all-black regiment that had fought in the Union Army during the Civil War. Much later, during World War I, Johnson again saw black men in uniform during a visit to Washington, D.C. Because of the rumors of German spies and pro-German Americans, the White House and the State Department were surrounded by troops. Every guard that Johnson saw was black. During Johnson's day and until long after, traditional thinking held that the Negro would never make a first-

class fighting man. Black soldiers and sailors were often relegated to
roles as stevedores or messmen or were segregated into black units
where they were commanded chiefly by white officers. Yet Johnson's
depiction of the black troops he remembers places them in positions
of honor and in posts of importance.

Johnson's memory of life at Atlanta University also attacks a stereotype without mentioning it specifically—the negative stereotype of
black sexual morality. In order to call on a woman student socially,
the male student at Atlanta had to file a written application which
then had to be initialed by either the dean or the president of the
university. After passing this hurdle, the young man was allowed a
twenty-minute visit under the eye of a chaperone. Nor did the imagi-
nations of the young men fly unfettered: Johnson recalls that dormi-
tory discussions of the opposite sex were characterized by extreme
idealism and that "realistic discussion of sex" was almost nonexistent
(A, 68). Morality at Atlanta was closely regulated in all areas. Students signed a pledge to abstain from alcohol, tobacco, and profanity,
and chapel attendance was required.

The idealism concerning women students extends to Johnson's
memory of their charms. Long before the "black is beautiful" movement of the 1960s, Johnson wrote a lyrical passage about the "taste-
fully dressed, good-mannered, good-looking girls" of Atlanta and
expressed the opinion that "there was a warmth of beauty in [their]
variety and blend of color and shade that no group of white girls
could kindle" (A, 75).

In Johnson's day Negroes were not popularly supposed to have the
capacity to occupy positions of responsibility, but Johnson frequently
calls the reader's attention to black people he saw in such positions.
As a boy in Jacksonville, he had known black policemen and firemen,
city councilmen, two justices of the peace, and a municipal judge as
well as many small businessmen. Later, on his travels through the
Caribbean and Central America, Johnson saw black clerks and accoun-
tants in Panama and black customs officials, policemen, soldiers, and
clerks in Jamaica.

Black contributions to American life of which Johnson reminds us
range from the athletic victories of Eddie Tolan and Ralph Metcalf in
the 1932 Olympic Games in Los Angeles to the artistic achievements
of black Americans in the fields of folktales, dance, and music. He
goes so far as to assert that "the only things in America that have
sprung from American soil, permeated American life, and been uni-

versally acknowledged as distinctly American, [have] been the creations of the American Negro" (*A, 327*).

Johnson on Education

Much of Johnson's mature life spanned the period when great controversy on education raged between the two major black leaders,
Booker T. Washington and W. E. B. DuBois. Washington's theory
was that education for black people should be built on a broad base,
that the first obligation of educators should be to see that large numbers of the Negro population were educated well enough to support
themselves and their families. True higher education at Washington's
Tuskegee Institute was neglected in favor of practical subjects that
would prepare students for jobs in agriculture or industry. DuBois,
who had studied at Harvard and the University of Berlin as well as
at Fisk University, propounded the "talented tenth" theory, which
held that the most gifted members of the race should be educated to
their full potential, after which they would help to pull the lower
classes up toward their level. Johnson had been friendly with both
men and had tactfully avoided taking sides in the debate between
them, but *Along This Way* suggests that his sympathies lay closer to
the DuBois position than to that of Washington.

Johnson admits that his parents were his greatest assets when it
came to education. His mother had been well educated at a school
for "colored" children in New York City, and his father, while self-
educated, had managed to teach himself enough so that he had a
working command of Spanish, an adequate ability to manage his own
investments, and a yearning for cultural activities such as reading and
theatergoing. Both Johnson and his brother received their first piano
lessons from their mother, and Johnson profited a great deal from the
presence of numerous books in the home as he was growing up, beginning with children's classics and progressing to the works of Dickens and Scott. Thus, the Johnson home was a far more positive
environment for education than the average nineteenth-century home,
black or white. In fact, Johnson's progress at home probably out-
stripped his progress at Stanton School, the poorly administered "colored" school to which Johnson's race consigned him. An implicit
point made in the early section of *Along This Way* is the importance
of a home environment that will favor education.

In Johnson's education Atlanta University was the turning point that he would look back on happily for the rest of his life. Although his father first preferred Hampton Institute, which stressed the sort of practical education advocated by its most famous graduate, Booker T. Washington, Johnson's mother favored Atlanta. Johnson became one of the student leaders of Atlanta in spite of the fact that, like many of its students, he had to enter as a preparatory student. Education at Atlanta ranged from languages—Latin and Greek as well as French and German—to practical training in manual arts such as woodworking and printing. Because he was "terror-stricken" when he was called upon to speak in public, Johnson forced himself to study oratory and to participate in extracurricular speech contests, training that would serve him well in later years. The message for black youths who read his autobiography was clear: the obstacles that appeared in one's way were to be regarded as challenges, and the greater the challenge, the greater should be the determination with which it would be attacked. Interestingly, the one challenge posed by Atlanta that Johnson did not accept with alacrity was the tradition of teaching in rural schools during the vacations. Johnson's experience of teaching at that level, while he treats it with humor, suggests that his sympathies were not with Booker T. Washington's approach to the completely uneducated.

Upon graduation, Johnson had an immediate chance to put his own theories of education to the test as the principal of his old school, Stanton. Remembering the failings of Stanton that he had discovered when he moved on to the Atlanta preparatory division, Johnson tailored the new high school courses that he initiated in such a way that Stanton graduates would be prepared to attend college, and he taught several of the new courses, such as Spanish, himself. Although his career in musical comedy eventually led him away from Stanton, Johnson remained vitally interested in education for the rest of his life, as a student taking classes part-time, as a member of the Board of Trustees of Atlanta University, and eventually as the first person to occupy the chair of creative writing at Fisk University.

Key ideas that emerge from his discussions of education in *Along This Way* are the importance of using one's spare time, the continuing nature of the educational process, and an implicit adherence to Du-Bois's principles of education. Johnson suggests that "an explanation . . . of whatever success that has come my way [is] my abhorrence of 'spare time' " (A, 192). This desire to fill his time with meaningful activity instead of mere diversion and his lifelong ambition for more education led him to avoid spare time by studying for the bar exams while principal of Stanton and by taking courses under Brander Matthews of Columbia while he worked in musical comedy. The limitations of Washington's narrow education were rejected, at least for those who were capable of mastering more.

Discrimination and Worse

Among the most important factors in Johnson's life, and in his account of how America looked to him over the years, were racial discrimination and the violence that he had experienced and witnessed. His early life in Jacksonville had been relatively free of racism, but as soon as he left for college he learned what black southerners had to contend with. His experience with Jim Crow regulations on the way to Atlanta could be laughed off because Johnson and his companion were in no real danger. In fact, he soon learned that laughter was a major weapon used by the black American to fight racism. During his first year at the university he noticed that his classmates laughed heartily at the slightest provocation, and he asked himself whether the habit hinted at "mental vacuity" or at a deep understanding of the irony of their lives. Finally he decided "that a part of this laughter, when among themselves, was laughter at the white man" (*A*, 120). In effect, he is both pointing out to black readers one of their own best defenses and at the same time making white readers aware of a complexity they have not suspected in black people.

Johnson had his own occasions to laugh at the white man. Once in Jacksonville he was taunted by a white man who asked him publicly what he would give to be a white man. When the laughter of the white crowd died down, Johnson topped the heckler's joke by replying, "I am sure that I wouldn't give anything to be the kind of white man you are. . . . I'd lose too much by the change" (*A*, 135). While these sound like fighting words, the young white realized that he had been beaten at his own game when he saw the reaction of the crowd. Johnson uses the incident, not to suggest that readers emulate his behavior, but to emphasize that he really never felt any desire to change places with a white man.

Many of the dangers Johnson and other black people faced could not be laughed off, however. The conductor on the train to Atlanta might be fooled by Johnson's impersonation of a foreigner, but on his first trip home from Atlanta a more serious situation developed. After again refusing to move to the Jim Crow car, Johnson saw that the white passengers in the first-class car were becoming increasingly threatening. Eventually, a friendly white man warned Johnson and his companions that the crew had telegraphed ahead to Baxley, Georgia, where a mob was being formed to board the train and take them off by force. Remembering it was at Baxley that a group of black ministers had been harassed and shot at, Johnson and his friends moved to the Jim Crow car.

Johnson treats not only the personal dangers that he occasionally faced, such as the encounter with angry militiamen mentioned earlier, but situations that went on around him. While working in New York with Rosamond during the summer of 1900, Johnson saw the results of a race riot. Barry Carter, a friend of the Johnsons who was caught out on the street, was beaten first by a white mob and later by the police officers to whom he fled for help. He was then jailed overnight before being released to seek medical attention. Carter did not die of the beating, but he never fully recovered his health. Later in the book Johnson further broadens his scope: his position with the NAACP made him aware of national incidents that did not touch him personally. He tells, for example, of one black soldier who returned from World War I and was lynched for no other reason than that he was wearing a U.S. Army uniform. Johnson contradicts the common white belief that lynching resulted from rapes committed by black men. Citing statistics gathered from the Library of Congress by NAACP researchers, he reports that of approximately three thousand lynchings which had taken place over a thirty-year period, only seventeen percent involved charges of rape. Other reasons were "talking back" to whites or failing to show exaggerated respect to them.

Johnson notes that some of his contemporaries have turned to violence or isolationism as solutions to the racial situation in the nation. He cites the example of Alonzo Jones of Jacksonville, who ordered a shipment of rifles and ammunition sufficient to arm a group of black citizens sworn to defend themselves if they were attacked. Soon after the rifles were delivered, some members of the black community did fire rifles to protect themselves during a riot, and when the incident was investigated, the rifles were traced to Jones. Although Jones escaped prison, he did so only by posting a high bond and then jumping bail. He lost all of his considerable property in Jacksonville and died a poor man. In Johnson's view, movements that isolate the Negro are as futile as Jones's armed resistance. However, for his white readers, Johnson's point in telling such stories is that the patience of black Americans is not unlimited, and he raises the possibility that armed confrontation may result if racial customs do not change.

Flight and laughter might avoid confrontations; fighting might simply make things worse. Johnson suggests by his example the sort of action he favors in dangerous situations. His behavior after the Jacksonville fire, when he was suspected of having a rendezvous with a white woman, is totally in character. His refusal to talk with the militiamen who arrested him and his demands to plead his case only before the provost marshal set an excellent example for black readers who might find themselves in similar dangerous situations. Johnson shows that neither abject capitulation nor defiance is necessary. Instead, a calm, dignified insistence on the observation of the law is the key not only to survival but to maintenance of one's self-respect.

His own major contribution to positive legal activity was his work on behalf of the Dyer Anti-Lynching Bill during the 1920s. Although his two years of work to promote the bill resulted in the passage of no new law, he remained convinced that such persistent legal campaigns would ultimately gain black Americans full equality under the law. The last pages of *Along This Way,* in which Johnson sums up the racial situation of 1930s, are a call for the same sort of steady pressure that he advocated during his years with the NAACP.

Johnson as Writer

While much of Johnson's energy was devoted to the pursuit of legal rights for his race, he is best remembered today for his literary creations. Thus *Along This Way* is valuable for its illumination of Johnson as a writer. The ruling principle that runs through Johnson's statements about his books and poems is that each must contribute in some way to the welfare of his race. The service ideal of Atlanta University helped to form his art as well as his public career. Although he tells of one experience with "artistic inspirations" that caused him to write his poem "Mother Night" at a single sitting after waking from a sound sleep, most of his works were produced in a sober and workmanlike manner, often with a deadline hanging over him. *Along This Way* offers information on the circumstances under which most of Johnson's works were composed and occasional insights into their meaning.

For example, "Lift Every Voice and Sing" was written for a celebration of Lincoln's birthday in 1900. Johnson had first planned a poem on Lincoln but was unable to complete it. As the time grew short, he turned to a song that could be sung by school children. Instead of focusing directly on Lincoln, it would emphasize the suffering the former slaves had endured and their hope for the future. Johnson "ground out" the first few lines of the poem in anything but an inspired state, but after finishing the first stanza, he was caught up by the ideas that were coming to him, and he completed the poem while he "paced back and forth on the front porch, repeating the lines over and over" (*A,* 154) with tears in his eyes. The lyrics expressed his beliefs about the plight and hopes of his race, and he always felt complimented when he found pirated, mimeographed copies of the song pasted into hymnals in black churches that he visited on later trips across the country. Knowing that the song spoke to and for his people was of greater value than the royalties that he might have received from the sheet music.

Johnson's role as writer for the stage might seem inappropriate for a man so dedicated to improving the image and lot of his race. The shows that Johnson, his brother Rosamond, and Bob Cole produced were humorous musical comedies that cast the Negro as a comic character who sang "coon songs" in dialect. But Johnson, without appearing apologetic, makes it clear that these shows also played their part in the struggle for black achievement. As the Johnson brothers and their partner discussed their writing, "the main question talked and wrangled over [was] always that of the manner and means of raising the status of the Negro as a writer, composer, and performer in the New York theater and world of music" (*A,* 172–73). Few black performers had appeared on Broadway at the turn of the century, and Johnson undoubtedly felt that it was desirable to have the Negro depicted by black actors and black writers even if both had to conform to some of the stereotypes created by white minstrels in blackface. Nor did Johnson simply follow the conventions of the theater as he found them. Eugene Levy notes that "the trio did not cater to the lowest levels of contemporary musical taste. In the hands of Cole and Johnson Brothers, coon song lyrics became noticeably more genteel."[6] As the demand for his services increased, Johnson used his power to persuade theater owner A. I. Erlanger to put a stop to the practices of a group, the Southern Society, that placed anti-Negro propaganda leaflets on theater seats before performances in an attempt to keep Negroes out of the theaters.

The Autobiography of an Ex-Colored Man has puzzled many readers, beginning with its first reviewers, and Johnson's comments in *Along This Way* indicate that the confusion of readers was no accident, that he meant to have the book accepted as a "human document." His reasoning in publishing the book anonymously is hinted at when he says that "the authorship of the book excited the curiosity of literate colored people, and there was speculation among them as to who the writer might be—to every such group some colored man who has married white, and so coincided with the main point on which the story turned, is known" (*A,* 238). His strategy was to engage the emotions of his readers more fully than he would have been able to do with an acknowledged work of fiction. Although he does not say so, he might also have hoped that literate white readers might wonder about the prevalence of "passing" and be disturbed by the implications of that social phenomenon.

Like "Lift Every Voice and Sing," "Fifty Years" was written with a deadline in mind. Johnson explains that he had intended to write a poem to commemorate the fiftieth anniversary of the Emancipation Proclamation. His duties in revolution-torn Nicaragua, however, distracted him, and he realized in October 1912 that the date of the Emancipation was at hand. In spite of the chaos at the embassy, where "one room in the Consulate was still used as marine headquarters [and] there were two machine guns on the front porch" (*A,* 290), Johnson wrote the poem in six weeks. Although as published it is an optimistic record of the progress of the black race in the United States and looks forward to further strides, the first draft of "Fifty Years" reflected Johnson's reservations about his country's treatment of its black citizens rather than his hopes for the future. Apparently he had to purge his system of the bitterness accumulated during countless rebuffs and humiliations before he could write the sort of public poem that "Fifty Years" was to be. During revision Johnson first moved the negative section of the poem to the end, and then, feeling that it was "artistically out of place, and, moreover, that it nullified the theme, purpose, and effect of the poem" (*A,* 290), he cut out the fifteen pessimistic stanzas completely.

Part of the story of his writing of *God's Trombones* has already been treated in chapter 3, but it is only in *Along This Way* that the reader comes to understand the whole creative process that produced Johnson's best book of poems. From the time he wrote "The Creation" to the time he finished the book seven years passed, during which Johnson not only compiled his collections of the spirituals but also, in his public role, fought for the passage of the Dyer Anti-Lynching Bill and documented cases of countless black victims who suffered the effects of racial violence. It was with those seven years as background that the rest of the book seemed to come together for Johnson. He tells how, on Thanksgiving Day of 1926, he sat down with an outline

for the second piece, "Go Down Death," and wrote the entire poem
before dinner. The balance of the book was ready to flow with equal
ease, and after a two-week stay at his vacation home near Great Bar-
rington, Massachusetts, following the Christmas of 1926, Johnson
finished *God's Trombones.*

The portrait of himself as artist that Johnson presents in *Along This
Way* is a self-consciously wrought one, as controlled as most of his
public statements about himself. The reader is always presented with
Johnson the artist of his people and never with the struggling artist
for whom disappointments and rage over his critical reception are up-
permost. However, in spite of the feeling that Johnson is always putting his best foot forward, the autobiography leaves the reader with a
sense of an engaging personality at work on a task that truly matters—the consolidation of the traditions of a race into an emerging
literary tradition.

A Word to White America

In the final pages of *Along This Way* Johnson looks forward rather
than backward: from the perspective of his long involvement with
race relations, he asks himself what he can tell his readers about the
future of his race and its relationship to the white majority. While
he addresses readers of both races in his conclusion, it is perhaps
to white America that his final words are primarily directed, for,
in addition to his predictions, his closing message includes a rhetori-
cal threat to the America that has excluded black people from full
participation.

Answering one question that had frequently been put to him,
Johnson concludes that the Negro will continue to progress. In spite
of the setbacks suffered because of the Depression during which he
was writing, he points to the major advances already made by the race
as evidence of its "ability to survive and advance under conditions and
obstacles that will [never] again be so hard" (A, 409). In spite of the
real barriers that remain for black citizens, Johnson asserts that the
white race has gradually become more fair in its attitude toward
the Negro, and further that it is in the interest of the white race to
end segregation. In the South especially, he suggests that it is folly to
burden taxpayers with the expense of "maintaining a dual educational
system, a dual railroad system, [and] dual public park systems" (A,
410). At the same time, it is "absurd" for the southern businessman
to bar a large number of potential customers from his place of busi-

ness in order to maintain segregation. Johnson's technique is nicely attuned to his white audience: first he compliments the race on its fairness and then he shows how continued segregation will affect the perpetrator financially.

As he would do in *Negro Americans, What Now?*, Johnson reassures the white reader that the Negro will not turn to communism, while at the same time he subtly suggests to black readers that it would be a great mistake to ally themselves with this "outlawed political and economic creed" (*A*, 411). He is equally reassuring to whites who fear the bugaboo of miscegenation when he advises them that for the most part the Negro has little interest in amalgamation of the races. However, he replaces the spectres of communism and miscegenation with a threat of his own. Denied his rightful place in American society, the Negro may embrace a philosophy of isolationism: "If the Negro is always to be given a heavy handicap back of the common scratch, or if the antagonistic forces are destined to dominate and bar all forward movement, there will be only one way of salvation for the race that I can see, and that will be through the making of its isolation into a religion and the cultivation of a hard, keen, relentless hatred for everything white" (*A*, 412). Johnson acknowledges that such a course would be extremely self-destructive, and deplores the fact that it might be adopted, but he also points out that "if the Negro is made to fall, America [will fall] with him" (*A*, 412). Again, self-interest should encourage white America to destroy the barriers between the races. His final word to white America insists that the racial problems of the nation must be dealt with quickly and incisively. They cannot, he says, be "met and answered by the mere mouthings of the worn platitudes of humanitarianism, of formal religion, or of abstract democracy. For the Negroes directly concerned are not in far-off Africa; they are in and within our midst" (*A*, 413).

Johnson ends his autobiography, then, with the most serious point that he has been making throughout the book. Black Americans have earned the right to full participation in American society, and they mean to have it. The engaging, warm, and often humorous character who emerges from the pages of *Along This Way*, the educator and writer who has spread his life before the reader, finally becomes subordinate to the political spokesman. Satisfying as it might have been to write a confessional autobiography, Johnson withstood the temptation and instead produced a political document in the tradition of the great black autobiographies.

Chapter Seven
Johnson's Lasting Contributions

James Weldon Johnson died on 26 June 1938, when his car was struck by a train at a railroad crossing near Wiscasset, Maine.[1] His funeral at Salem Methodist Church in Harlem was a tribute to his social and literary popularity. A large crowd heard tributes to Johnson from speakers such as Mayor Fiorello LaGuardia and former colleagues J. E. Spingarn and Walter White of the NAACP. In September the *Crisis* published a memorial issue, and the following year Fisk University issued a memorial brochure containing a brief biography, a bibliography, and essays ranging from personal statements by old friends Arthur Spingarn and Carl Van Vechten to a critical essay by Sterling A. Brown.[2] Contradicting the majority opinion that Johnson had been the foremost black man of letters of his time, however, was black historian Kelly Miller. Writing in his column in the *New York Age* less than a month after Johnson's death, Miller expressed the opinion that Johnson was a "literary dilettante scribbling prose or verse as the mode or the occasion required." His popularity, Miller suggested, was greater among members of the white race than within his own and was based on the fact that "he uttered nothing base or offensive to their racial sensibility."[3] Such comments make it necessary to consider just what Johnson's permanent contributions to black literature were.

Although a number of factors kept Johnson from devoting a great deal of time to any single genre, an overview of Afro-American literature since his time provides evidence that he excelled in two fields, fiction and poetry. *The Autobiography of an Ex-Colored Man,* largely ignored by the literary world when it was first published in 1912, came to be one of the most influential books of the Harlem Renaissance upon its republication in 1927: not only writers of the 1920s but novelists of the 1950s and later must acknowledge a debt to Johnson. As a poet and editor of poetry anthologies, he helped to move black poetry away from the genteel traditions of the nineteenth century and from the limiting clichés of dialect verse into new and productive modes that are still serving black poets well. Not only did he break away from old-fashioned "poetic diction" in *God's Trombones,* but by using the black southern preacher as his speaker he explored areas of oral folk expression that are still providing a poetic idiom for Afro-American poets.

The Influence of *The Autobiography*

The most immediate influence of Johnson's only novel on later black novelists came at nearly the same time that it was first being introduced to the general reading public. During the Harlem Renaissance the increasing interest in Afro-American literature led to the writing of three new novels on the theme of passing, all of which owe something to *The Autobiography.* Unlike earlier passing novels, Walter White's *Flight* (1926), Jessie Fauset's *Plum Bun* (1928), and Nella Larsen's *Passing* (1929) all attempt—with varying success—to leave melodrama behind in favor of psychological exploration, just as Johnson had done in 1912. Both White and Fauset knew *The Autobiography* from its 1912 edition, White because he had been serving as Johnson's assistant in the NAACP and Fauset because she had reviewed the novel for the *Crisis.* Because of interest during the 1920s in the exotic and the primitive, these three novels sold, but, as Robert A. Bone has observed, White, Fauset, and Larsen have little to add to Johnson's mature treatment of the psychology of passing and indeed reach back to earlier and more melodramatic treatments as well as to Johnson. Aptly, Bone classifies the three novelists of the 1920s as members of a "rear guard."[4]

More significant has been Johnson's influence on much later black novelists such as Ralph Ellison and James Baldwin. Parallels between *The Autobiography* and *Invisible Man* were discussed by critics during the 1970s. Both the ex-colored man and the invisible man are nameless protagonists; both are engaged in a search for identity; both see the world through a sort of double vision, as white man and black man; both are troubled by bouts of self-hatred; both are befriended by white liberals whose motives are suspect; and both novels take on a picaresque form as the protagonist travels widely in search of his identity as a black man and as an American.[5] While Ellison's is a complex novel, full of many allusions to works of American and world literature, his debts to Johnson are greater than the debts to any other

black American author, with the possible exception of Richard
Wright, whose "Man Who Lived Underground" is used along with
The Autobiography to give an underlying form and structure to *Invisible
Man*. Clearly, Ellison considered *The Autobiography* an important
milestone in the history of the Afro-American novel.

Although the affinities between *Invisible Man* and *The Autobiography*
are the most important evidence of the continuing influence of the
earlier novel simply because of the sheer number of thematic ties between Johnson and Ellison, many other later black novelists also build
on themes first treated by Johnson. Besides Ellison, the most famous
of these writers is James Baldwin. Baldwin explores two of the
themes used by Johnson in *The Autobiography*: racial self-hatred and
suspicion of the white patron/liberal. Like Johnson's ex-colored man,
who equates his blackness with uncleanness, Baldwin's John Grimes
is depicted as a boy obsessed with the pervasiveness of dirt in his environment. From his surname, Grimes, to various facets of his life—
sweeping and dusting the living room, enveloped in a cloud of dust,
walking the filthy streets or looking at the dirty cracked paint of his
apartment, and even writhing on the dirty threshing floor during his
conversion—John is surrounded by filth as if it were a badge of his
blackness. Like the ex-colored man, who is "scrubbed until his skin
ached" in childhood, John connects his skin color with impurity.
Baldwin echoes Johnson's protagonist's white father and his millionaire patron in the creation of several ambiguous white characters,
from the vaguely delineated white principal and the old white man
in the park in *Go Tell It on the Mountain* to Eric Jones of *Another
Country,* who loves Rufus Scott but exploits him sexually. While
Baldwin never echoes Johnson's novel as distinctly and allusively as
Ellison does, he has obviously been affected by it.

Minor influences of *The Autobiography of an Ex-Colored Man* are apparent in the works of other modern novelists, including Richard
Wright, William Demby, Chester Himes, Ann Petry, and John A.
Williams. Among the themes introduced by Johnson and followed up
by later authors are the love-hate relationship between black men and
their mothers; expatriation as a solution to the American racial dilemma, especially for black artists and writers; the conflict between
the materialistic values of the white society and the more human
values of black people; and the debate over the effectiveness of an
assimilationist course of action versus militant confrontation.

After a period of neglect, the popular and critical attitude toward

The Autobiography turned positive in the 1960s, beginning with its reprinting by Hill and Wang in 1960 and by Avon in 1965. These paperback editions, like the Knopf printing of 1927, came at a propitious time, for America was entering a new era of interest in Afro-American literature and culture. The 1970s saw rising interest in the novel as critics began to probe beneath the sociological surface to discover psychological complexities that earlier readers had overlooked. Johnson's skillful manipulation of his unreliable narrator to treat the complex ironies inherent in American racial attitudes and to depict the psychological ambivalence of his protagonist impresses today's readers as highly sophisticated, more akin to the work of contemporary novelists than to that of writers of Johnson's own day. Although he wrote only a single novel, Johnson's skill and perception have assured him a secure reputation in the history of Afro-American fiction.

Johnson's Contribution to Poetry

While the poems of *Fifty Years* were competent performances for their day and deserve some measure of recognition in Afro-American literary history, it is Johnson's free verse that has been acknowledged as his most original and affecting poetry. *God's Trombones* not only achieves what he intended by capturing the manner and rhetoric of the old-time black preacher, but taps a wellspring of innovative imagery and creates a new poetic idiom with tremendous power. Few readers can forget the emotional impact engendered by "The Prodigal Son" or "Go Down Death." Like Walt Whitman's "When Lilacs Last in the Dooryard Bloom'd," the poems of *God's Trombones* become a part of the reader's own experience. It was with these free-verse poems that Johnson made a lasting contribution upon which later black poets could build. But while discussions of *God's Trombones* appear in critical surveys, duly acknowledged as part of that literary phenomenon known as the Harlem Renaissance, recognition of their true worth has lagged behind that accorded to *The Autobiography* as seminal fiction.

One reason for this lack of recognition is the fact that, unlike the situation in the novel, no great works of poetry by later black poets show distinct allusions to *God's Trombones* parallel to Ellison's allusions to *The Autobiography*. Religion is not such an important theme in black poetry as it once was; only scattered poems by important poets closely follow the stylistic example of *God's Trombones* while treating related subject matter. Nevertheless, a partial listing of some poems that definitely show the influence of Johnson would include works such as Margaret Walker's "Micah," which uses biblical imagery and the style of the black preacher's sermon to praise the late Medgar Evers; Owen Dodson's "Black Mother Praying," whose idiom and imagery reflect Johnson's; David Henderson's "Pentecostal Sunday: A Song of Power," which employs the language of the Christian preacher, while coming to a different conclusion; James Emanuel's "To a Negro Preacher," which similarly denies the power of religion while reminding the reader of the black preacher's power with words; and Mari Evans's "Speak the Truth to the People," which uses the rhetoric of the preacher for secular ends.

More important than this most direct influence on later poetry, however, is the general influence that Johnson's experiments had on later black poets. Johnson was one of a small group—also including Langston Hughes and Sterling A. Brown—that helped to establish the language of black poetry in the later twentieth century. As Johnson noted in his introduction to *The Book of American Negro Poetry,* dialect of the sort that he and Dunbar had written at or before the turn of the century was no longer acceptable by the time of the Harlem Renaissance. Johnson used the language of the black church, Hughes the language of jazz and the blues, and Brown that of blues and folktales to set up alternative representations of the vernacular that would serve later poets. Horrified as the genteel Johnson might be to read Don L. Lee's "Don't Cry, Scream" or Larry Neal's "Morning Raga for Malcolm," his experiments with the black idiom helped to make such poems possible.

Like *The Autobiography,* both *God's Trombones* and *The Book of American Negro Poetry* returned to print in the 1960s as a result of the increased interest in Afro-American art during that decade. Both appeared in paperback editions, *God's Trombones* being published by Viking and *American Negro Poetry* by Harcourt, Brace. The two readily accessible works have brought praise from critics as diverse as Bernard W. Bell, whose *Folk Roots of Contemporary Afro-American Poetry* was published by the iconoclastic Broadside Press, and academics such as Blyden Jackson and Louis D. Rubin, Jr., whose *Black Poetry in America* was issued by a university press.[6] Eugene Redmond called *God's Trombones* not only Johnson's masterpiece, but one of the best books of Afro-American poetry,[7] while C. W. E. Bigsby has recently noted its influence on writers of the "second black renaissance" of the 1950s

through the 1970s.[8] Johnson's contributions to black life and literature were acknowledged in 1971 by special issues of *Phylon* and the
Crisis on the centennial anniversary of his birth.[9]

Johnson, then, has had a lasting impact upon Afro-American literature in spite of his failure to concentrate on a single genre and to
master it thoroughly. Like Paul Laurence Dunbar and Charles W.
Chesnutt, he wrote during difficult times and had to shape his career
to those times. Unlike either of these contemporaries, Johnson had a
major political impact on the future of his race and pursued his literary career as an avocation for most of his life. The two minor master-
pieces of that effort, *The Autobiography of an Ex-Colored Man* and *God's
Trombones,* remain provocative and influential books.

Notes and References

Chapter One

1. *Along This Way: The Autobiography of James Weldon Johnson* (New York: Viking Press, 1933), 11–13; hereafter cited in parentheses in the text as *A* with page number.
2. Eugene Levy, *James Weldon Johnson: Black Leader, Black Voice* (Chicago and London: University of Chicago Press, 1973), 15.
3. For an account of the background of Atlanta University, see Levy, *Johnson*, 25–31, Myron Adams, *A History of Atlanta University* (Atlanta: Atlanta University Press, 1930), and Clarence A. Bacote, *The Story of Atlanta University* (Atlanta: Atlanta University Press, 1969).
4. Levy, *Johnson*, 40–41.
5. Ernest C. Tate, "Sentiment and Horse Sense: James Weldon Johnson's Style," *Negro History Bulletin* 25 (April 1962):152.
6. Levy, *Johnson*, 44.
7. See *Along This Way*, 229 and Levy, *Johnson*, 109 for slightly different accounts of the fire and its aftermath.
8. *Daily American.* Clipping in James Weldon Johnson Scrapbook 1, p. 17, James Weldon Johnson Collection, Beinecke Library, Yale University. Future references to *Daily American* are cited in the text by scrapbook page number.
9. "Views and Reviews," *New York Age*, 22 October 1914. Scrapbook, James Weldon Johnson Collection, Beinecke Library, Yale University. Future references to the *New York Age* are cited by date within the text.

Chapter Two

1. *The Autobiography of an Ex-Coloured Man* (New York: Alfred A. Knopf, 1927), 43. Except for the consistent use of British spellings (e.g., "coloured" for "colored") this text is identical with the Sherman, French edition, currently virtually unavailable to most readers. The Hill & Wang paperback reprint reproduces the Knopf edition. Future references are to this edition and are cited in parentheses in the text.
2. Levy, *Johnson*, 16–17.
3. Ibid., 62–63.
4. Both the autograph manuscript and typescript are in the James Weldon Johnson Collection, Beinecke Library, Yale University.
5. Jessie Fauset, *Crisis* 5 (November 1912):38.
6. Sterling A. Brown, "A Century of Negro Portraiture in American Literature," *Massachusetts Review* 7 (Winter 1966):82.

7. In *Along This Way,* 238, Johnson tells how his brother Rosamond suggested *The Chameleon* as a title: "I also debated with myself the aptness of *The Autobiography of an Ex-Colored Man* as a title. Brander Matthews had expressed a liking for the title, but my brother had thought it was clumsy and too long; he had suggested *The Chameleon.* In the end, I stuck to the original idea of issuing the book without the author's name, and kept the title that had appealed to me first. But I have never been able to settle definitely for myself whether I was sagacious or not in these two decisions. When I chose the title, it was without the slightest doubt that its meaning would be perfectly clear to anyone; there were people, however, to whom it proved confusing."

Chapter Three

1. *Fifty Years and Other Poems* (Boston: Cornhill Co., 1917), 22; hereafter cited in parentheses in the text as *FY* with page number.

2. *New York Times,* 1 January 1913, p. 16, columns 5–6.

3. *St. Peter Relates an Incident: Selected Poems* (New York: Viking Press, 1935), 101; hereafter cited in parentheses in the text as *SP* with page number.

4. *Bulletin of Atlanta University,* no. 44 (March 1893):1.

5. However, Richard Long, in "A Weapon of My Song: The Poetry of James Weldon Johnson," *Phylon* 32 (Winter 1971):377, feels it necessary to defend the inclusion of "The White Witch" in the category of "race" poems.

6. *God's Trombones: Seven Negro Sermons in Verse* (New York: Viking Press, 1927), 6–7; hereafter cited in parentheses in the text as *GT* with page number.

7. *Along This Way,* 336–37. See also Levy, *Johnson,* 306.

8. William Stanley Braithwaite, "The Poems of James Weldon Johnson," *Boston Evening Transcript,* 12 December 1917, part 2, p. 9.

9. Benjamin Brawley, review of *Fifty Years and Other Poems, Journal of Negro History* 3 (April 1918):202–3.

10. Maya Angelou, *I Know Why the Caged Bird Sings* (New York: Random House, 1969), 178–79.

11. Harriet Monroe, "Negro Sermons," *Poetry: A Magazine of Verse* 30 (August 1927):29.

12. "Poetry and Eloquence of the Negro Preacher," *New York Times Book Review,* 19 June 1927, p. 11.

13. Thomas Munroe, "The Grand Manner in Negro Poetry: *God's Trombone {sic},*" *New York Herald Tribune Books,* 5 June 1927, p. 3.

14. Joseph Auslander, "Sermon Sagas," *Opportunity* 5 (September 1927):274–75.

15. Countee Cullen, "And the Walls Came Tumblin' Down," *Bookman* 66 (October 1927):221–22.

16. W. E. B. DuBois, "The Browsing Reader," *Crisis* 34 (July 1927):159; Alain Locke, "The Negro Poet and His Tradition," *Survey* 58 (1 August 1927):473–74.

17. Wallace Thurman, "Negro Poets and Their Poetry," *Bookman* 67 (July 1928):555–61.

18. Eugene B. Redmond, *Drumvoices: A Critical History* (Garden City, N.Y.: Doubleday, 1976), 187, 189.

19. Arthur P. Davis, *From the Dark Tower: Afro-American Writers, 1900 to 1960* (Washington, D.C.: Howard University Press, 1974), 29.

20. Blyden Jackson and Louis D. Rubin, Jr., *Black Poetry in America: Two Essays in Historical Interpretation* (Baton Rouge, La.: Louisiana State University Press, 1974), 26.

Chapter Four

1. "The Creative Negro," in *America as Americans See It,* ed. Fred J. Ringel (New York: Harcourt, Brace & Co., 1932), 161.

2. *The Book of American Negro Poetry* (New York: Harcourt, Brace & World, 1959), 9; hereafter cited in parentheses in the text as *BNP* with page number.

3. See Levy, *Johnson,* 307.

4. *The Book of American Negro Spirituals* (New York: Viking Press, 1925), 19; hereafter cited in parentheses in the text as *BNS* with page number.

5. "Negro Authors and White Publishers," *Crisis* 36 (July 1929): 229.

6. "The Dilemma of the Negro Author," *American Mercury* 15 (1928):477.

7. Sterling A. Brown, "Negro Character as Seen by White Authors," *Journal of Negro Education* 2 (January 1933):179–201.

8. "Dilemma of the Negro Author," 479.

9. Ibid., 481.

10. Ibid.

11. "Race Prejudice and the Negro Artist," *Harper's Monthly Magazine* 157 (1928):775.

12. Ibid., 776.

Chapter Five

1. Levy, *Johnson,* 287–90.

2. "The Making of Harlem," *Survey Graphic* 6, no. 6 (March 1925):639.

3. Ibid.

4. *Black Manhattan* (New York: Arno Press and *New York Times,* 1968), vii. A reprint of the 1930 edition; this is cited hereafter in parentheses in the text as *BM* with page number.

5. Levy, *Johnson*, 323–24.

6. *Negro Americans, What Now?* (New York: Viking Press, 1938), 12; hereafter cited in parentheses in the text as *NA* with page number.

7. W. E. B. DuBois, "James Weldon Johnson Sings Praise of Negroes' Mecca," *New York Evening Post*, 12 July 1930, section 3, p. 5.

8. W. E. B. DuBois, "Whither Bound, Negroes?" *New York Herald Tribune Books*, 18 November 1934, p. 4.

Chapter Six

1. James Weldon Johnson Collection, Beinecke Library, Yale University, item 110.

2. Ibid., item 111 b.

3. Ibid., item 110.

4. Ibid.

5. Ibid.

6. Levy, *Johnson*, 87–88.

Chapter Seven

1. Levy, *Johnson*, 346. "Negro Leader Dies in Crossing Crash," *New York Times*, 27 June 1938, p. 17.

2. *Crisis* 45 (September 1938). Department of Publicity, Fisk University, *James Weldon Johnson* (Nashville, Tenn.: Fisk University).

3. Kelly Miller, "Kelly Miller writes About: James Weldon Johnson The Negro Poet Laureate," *New York Age*, 9 January 1938, p. 6.

4. Robert A. Bone, *The Negro Novel in America* (New Haven and London: Yale University Press, 1968), 95–107.

5. Robert E. Fleming, "Contemporary Themes in Johnson's *Autobiography of an Ex-Colored Man*," *Negro American Literature Forum* 4 (Winter 1970):120–24, 141, and Houston A. Baker, Jr., "A Forgotten Prototype: *The Autobiography of An Ex-Colored Man* and *Invisible Man*" in his *Singers of Daybreak* (Washington, D.C.: Howard University Press, 1974), 17–31.

6. Bernard W. Bell, "Folk Art and the Harlem Renaissance," in his *The Folk Roots of Contemporary Afro-American Poetry* (Detroit: Broadside Press, 1974), 27–31. Jackson and Rubin, "The Search for a Language, 1746–1923," in their *Black Poetry in America*, 1–36.

7. Redmond, *Drumvoices*, 184–89.

8. C. W. E. Bigsby, *The Second Black Renaissance: Essays in Black Literature* (Westport, Conn.: Greenwood Press, 1980), 261–62.

9. *Phylon* 32 (Winter 1971); *Crisis* 78 (June 1971).

Selected Bibliography

PRIMARY SOURCES

1. Books

Along This Way. New York: Viking Press, 1933.
The Autobiography of an Ex-Colored Man. Boston: Sherman French, 1912. Reprint. *The Autobiography of an Ex-Coloured Man.* New York: Knopf, 1927.
Black Manhattan. New York: Knopf, 1930.
The Book of American Negro Poetry. New York: Harcourt, Brace, 1922. Rev. ed., 1931.
The Book of American Negro Spirituals. New York: Viking Press, 1925.
Fifty Years and Other Poems. Boston: Cornhill, 1917.
God's Trombones. New York: Viking Press, 1927.
Negro Americans, What Now? New York: Viking Press, 1934.
The Second Book of American Negro Spirituals. New York: Viking Press, 1926.
St. Peter Relates an Incident. New York: Viking Press, 1930. A limited edition of 200 copies, privately distributed. Reprint. *St. Peter Relates an Incident: Selected Poems.* New York: Viking Press, 1935.

2. Shorter Writings

"A Brand" [poem]. *Bulletin of Atlanta University,* no. 44 (March 1893):1.
"The Contribution of the Negro." In *Our Racial and Cultural Minorities,* ed. Francis J. Brown and Joseph Slabey Roucek, 739–48. New York: Prentice-Hall, 1939.
"The Creative Negro." In *America as Americans See It,* ed. Fred J. Ringel, 160–65. New York: Harcourt, Brace, 1932.
"The Dilemma of the Negro Author." *American Mercury* 15 (1928):477–81.
"Futility" [poem]. *Harper's Monthly Magazine* 159 (1929):699.
"The Making of Harlem." *Survey Graphic* 6 (1925):635–39.
"Negro Authors and White Publishers." *Crisis* 36 (1929): 228–29.
"Race Prejudice and the Negro Artist." *Harper's Monthly Magazine* 157 (1928):769–76.
"What Atlanta University Has Done for Me." *Bulletin of Atlanta University,* no. 64 (April 1895):2.

3. Manuscript Materials

James Weldon Johnson Memorial Collection, Beinecke Rare Book Room and Manuscript Library, Yale University, New Haven, Connecticut.

SECONDARY SOURCES

1. Bibliography

Fleming, Robert E. *James Weldon Johnson and Arna Wendell Bontemps: A Reference Guide,* 3–67. Boston: G. K. Hall, 1978. Annotates secondary sources, 1905–1976.

2. Biographical and Critical Sources

Baker, Houston A., Jr. "A Forgotten Prototype: *The Autobiography of an Ex-Colored Man* and *Invisible Man.*" *Virginia Quarterly Review* 49 (1973):433–49. Reprinted in his *Singers of Daybreak: Studies in Black American Literature.* Washington, D.C.: Howard University Press, 1974. Treats *The Autobiography* as an important influence on Ellison's *Invisible Man* and draws a number of specific parallels between the two novels.

Bone, Robert A. "Novels of the Talented Tenth" in his *The Negro Novel in America,* rev. ed., 45–49. New Haven and London: Yale University Press, 1965. Sees Johnson as the best of the early black novelists, primarily because of his skillful use of irony.

Brawley, Benjamin. "Protest and Vindication" in his *The Negro Genius,* 206–14. New York: Dodd, Mead & Co., 1937. Brief biographical summary and overview of Johnson's work, with emphasis on his poetry, which Brawley sees as his greatest achievement.

Butterfield, Stephen. *Black Autobiography in America.* Amherst, Mass.: University of Massachusetts Press, 1974. Discussions of the common features of black autobiography, with frequent references to *Along This Way.*

Carroll, Richard A. "Black Racial Spirit: An Analysis of James Weldon Johnson's Critical Perspective." *Phylon* 32 (1971):344–64. Johnson's principles as a critic of black poetry.

Collier, Eugenia W. "The Endless Journey of an Ex-Coloured Man." *Phylon* 32 (1971):365–73. Draws parallels between the physical journeys of the ex-colored man and his psychological journey from one race to another and back again.

————. "James Weldon Johnson: Mirror of Change." *Phylon* 21 (1960):351–59. Traces Johnson's transition from dialect poetry to the new poetic idiom he created for *God's Trombones.*

Faulkner, Howard. "James Weldon Johnson's Portrait of the Artist as Invisible Man." *Black American Literature Forum* 19 (1985):147–51. Considers the novel's portrait of the narrator as one who fails to live his life fully and compares to *Invisible Man.*

Fleming, Robert E. "The Composition of James Weldon Johnson's 'Fifty Years.'" *American Poetry* 4, no. 2 (1987):51–56. Examines manuscript of "Fifty Years" and prints stanzas omitted in final draft of poem.

————. "Contemporary Themes in Johnson's *Autobiography of an Ex-Coloured*

Man." *Negro American Literature Forum* 4 (1970):120–24, 141. Examination of Johnson's influence on later Afro-American novelists such as Ralph Ellison, James Baldwin, Richard Wright, and Ann Petry.

————. "Irony as a Key to Johnson's *The Autobiography of an Ex-Coloured Man.*" *American Literature* 43 (1971):83–96. Analysis of Johnson's use of the unreliable narrator to achieve irony.

Garrett, Marvin P. "Early Recollections and Structural Irony in *The Autobiography of an Ex-Coloured Man.*" *Critique: Studies in Modern Fiction* 13 (1971):5–14. Study of the ironic level of the novel with emphasis on the clues to the narrator's character in chapter 2.

Gloster, Hugh M. "James Weldon Johnson" in his *Negro Voices in American Fiction,* 79–83. Chapel Hill: University of North Carolina Press, 1948. Credits Johnson with inspiring many novelists of the Harlem Renaissance, particularly Walter White, Nella Larsen, and Jessie Fauset.

Jackson, Blyden, and Louis D. Rubin, Jr. "The Search for a Language, 1746–1923" in their *Black Poetry in America: Two Essays in Historical Interpretation,* 1, 3–4, 14–15, 19–31, 35–36. Baton Rouge: Louisiana State University Press, 1974. Emphasizes Johnson's search for a new idiom for black poetry, through literary English and dialect and culminating in the free-verse poems of *God's Trombones.*

Jackson, Miles M., Jr. "Letters to a Friend: Correspondence from James Weldon Johnson to George A. Towns." *Phylon* 29 (1968):182–98. Quotes and reprints letters written to Johnson's former roommate between 1896 and 1934.

Levy, Eugene. *James Weldon Johnson: Black Leader, Black Voice.* Chicago: University of Chicago Press, 1973. The standard biography of Johnson, including a checklist of Johnson's publications.

Long, Richard A. "A Weapon of My Song: The Poetry of James Weldon Johnson." *Phylon* 32 (1971):374–82. Discusses both form and content of Johnson's poetry, which moves from standard English poems to free verse and from accommodation to militance.

O'Sullivan, Maurice J., Jr. "Of Souls and Pottage: James Weldon Johnson's *The Autobiography of an Ex-Coloured Man.*" *CLA Journal* 23 (1979):60–70. Treats Johnson's portrayal of his protagonist as more sympathetic than has generally been acknowledged. Neither hero nor villain, the ex-colored man is seen simply as a marginal man, unable to resolve his feelings of ambivalence.

Ovington, Mary White. "James Weldon Johnson, 1920–1931; We Meet the Nation" in her *The Walls Came Tumbling Down,* 176–243. New York: Harcourt, Brace, 1947. History of Johnson's role as Secretary of the NAACP.

Redding, J. Saunders. *To Make a Poet Black,* 87–89, 96–97, 120–22. Chapel Hill: University of North Carolina Press, 1939. Examines Johnson's poetry as part of the "New Negro" movement.

Rosenblatt, Roger. *Black Fiction,* 173–84. Cambridge, Mass.: Harvard

University Press, 1974. Praises *The Autobiography* for its psychological complexity.

Ross, Stephen M. "Audience and Irony in Johnson's *The Autobiography of an Ex-Coloured Man.*" *CLA Journal* 18 (1974):198–210. Argues that the irony in *The Autobiography* is directed at the white world, not at the narrator himself.

Skerrett, Joseph T., Jr. "Irony and Symbolic Action in James Weldon Johnson's *The Autobiography of an Ex-Coloured Man.*" *American Quarterly* 32 (1980):540–58. Compares *The Autobiography* and *Along This Way* to determine where the novel is ironic and where it is tragic, using a psychological approach.

Stepto, Robert B. *From Behind the Veil: A Study of Afro-American Narrative,* 95–127. Urbana, Ill.: University of Illinois Press, 1979. Analyzes Johnson's novel as a fictional modification of the Afro-American narrative tradition, from slave narrative through autobiography.

Tate, Ernest C. "Sentiment and Horse Sense: James Weldon Johnson's Style." *Negro History Bulletin* 25 (1962):152–54. Deals with Johnson's ability as a humorist; reprints a letter and poem sent to Rosamond Johnson while James Weldon Johnson was teaching in Georgia.

Thomas, Ruth Marie. "Author, Diplomat, and Public Servant: A Study of James Weldon Johnson's Writings." *Southwestern Journal* 5 (1949):58–72. Emphasizes the "humanitarian" content of Johnson's published works.

Vauthier, Simone. "The Interplay of Narrative Modes in James Weldon Johnson's *The Autobiography of an Ex-Colored Man.*" *Jährbuch für Amerikastudien* 18 (1973):173–81. Suggests that while *The Autobiography* seems to be written in the autobiographical mode, it actually is a picaresque novel in which Johnson satirizes the American dream.

Wagner, Jean. *Black Poets of the United States,* 351–84. Translated by Kenneth Douglas. Urbana, Ill.: University of Illinois Press, 1973. (Originally published as *Les Poetes Negres des Etats-Unis.* Paris: Librairie Istra, 1962.) Traces the growth of Johnson's poetic form and emphasizes how he was torn between the desire to entertain and the desire to protest in the content of his poetry.

Whalum, Wendell Phillips. "James Weldon Johnson's Theories and Performance Practices of Afro-American Folksong." *Phylon* 32 (1971):383–95. Study of Johnson as collector and critic of spirituals.

Index